TOBY WALSH is one of the world's leading experts in artificial intelligence, and has spent his life dreaming about and researching how machines might think. He is Scientia Professor of AI at the University of New South Wales and a Fellow of the Australian Academy of Science. Toby is a passionate advocate for limits that ensure AI is used to improve, not hurt, our lives. His last book, *It's Alive! Artificial Intelligence from the Logic Piano to Killer Robots*, was named by the *New Statesman* as one of its books of the year. Toby is a regular contributor to *American Scientist*, *New Scientist* and *The Guardian*.

PRAISE FOR *2062*

'As Toby Walsh convincingly puts it, "the golden age of philosophy is just about to begin" – a testament to both the richness and the urgency of the questions that confront us between now and 2062. This is a compelling invitation to imagine the future we want, and a lively provocation to make it happen.'
—**Brian Christian**, author of *The Most Human Human* and co-author of *Algorithms to Live By*

'If you want to explore what the disruptive future shaped by AI could be, read this book.'
—**James Canton**, CEO of the Institute for Global Futures and author of *Future Smart*

'One day, machines will surpass humans in all forms of general intelligence. When will that happen? The answer, according to a survey of experts, is the year 2062. If you want to read a lively and well-informed speculation about what could happen next, you can't do better than Toby Walsh's amazing new book.'
—**Erik Brynjolfsson**, professor at MIT and co-author of *The Second Machine Age*

'Clarity and sanity in a world full of fog and uncertainty – a timely book about the race to remain human.'
—**Richard Watson**, author of *Digital VS Human* and futurist-in-residence at the Imperial College, London

'"What happens next?" is the question that drives human curiosity and innovation. In *2062*, Walsh asks that question of one of the most critical junctures on our horizon – the point at which machines become as intelligent as humans. If you're looking for a road map to help navigate that future, look no further.'
—**Joel Werner**, broadcaster and science journalist

'One of the deepest questions facing humanity, pondered by a mind well and truly up to the task. Rip in!'
—**Adam Spencer**, broadcaster

2062

THE WORLD THAT AI MADE

TOBY WALSH

LA TROBE
UNIVERSITY PRESS

IN CONJUNCTION WITH BLACK INC.

Published by La Trobe University Press in conjunction with Black Inc.
Level 1, 221 Drummond Street
Carlton VIC 3053, Australia
enquiries@blackincbooks.com
www.blackincbooks.com
www.latrobeuniversitypress.com.au

La Trobe University plays an integral role in Australia's public intellectual life, and
is recognised globally for its research excellence and commitment to ideas and debate.
La Trobe University Press publishes books of high intellectual quality, aimed at general
readers. Titles range across the humanities and sciences, and are written by distinguished
and innovative scholars. La Trobe University Press books are produced in conjunction
with Black Inc., an independent Australian publishing house. The members of the LTUP
Editorial Board are Vice-Chancellor's Fellows Emeritus Professor Robert Manne and
Dr Elizabeth Finkel, and Morry Schwartz and Chris Feik of Black Inc.

9781760640514 (paperback)
9781743820254 (ebook)

A catalogue record for this
book is available from the
National Library of Australia

Cover design by Kim Ferguson
Text design and typesetting by Marilyn de Castro
Printed in Australia by McPherson's Printing Group

MIX
Paper from
responsible sources
FSC® C001695

To A and B,
who make my life so complete

CONTENTS

0001

HOMO DIGITALIS

Humans are remarkable. Indeed, despite the abundance of life on the planet, we are perhaps the *most* remarkable species ever to inhabit it. We have reversed rivers, built islands and generally bent nature to our ways. We have constructed buildings that amaze. The monumental pyramids at Giza. The sprawling Great Wall of China. The stunning Sagrada Família.[1] We have crossed the hottest deserts, and climbed the highest mountains. We have sent a roadster into space. We have even left the Earth to walk on the Moon.

We have created scientific theories that explain the mysteries of the universe – from milliseconds after its birth 13 billion years ago, until its eventual death 1 googol years in the future.[2] We have tamed fire, eradicated smallpox and banded together to overthrow despots and dictators. We have created art so sublime that it moves people to tears. The glorious melodies of Bach's St Matthew Passion. The naked beauty of Michelangelo's David. The haunting sadness of the Taj Mahal.

But despite all these marvellous achievements, we will soon be replaced. Almost all traces of *Homo sapiens* will be erased from the Earth, just like almost all traces of our predecessor *Homo neanderthalensis* have gone. For evolution never stops.

Around 50,000 years ago, *Homo neanderthalensis* was no match for the rise of *Homo sapiens*. We don't know precisely when or how the Neanderthals died out. It might have been their failure to adapt to a changing climate – a problem that ought to echo loudly to us today. Or it might be that *Homo sapiens* outcompeted them and left them no ecological niche in which to survive.

Whatever it was, the Neanderthals clearly did die out, and were replaced by us. Like every species before us, we too will be replaced by a new and more successful one. And as we're smart – don't forget that sapiens, or 'wise', is actually part of our species name – we can even predict who that successor will be.

Our successor is *Homo digitalis* – the evolution of the genus *Homo* into digital form. Both what we do and where we do it will become increasingly, and in some cases exclusively, digital. Human thought will be replaced by digital thought. And human activity in the real world will be supplanted by digital activity in artificial and virtual worlds. This is our artificially intelligent future.

My last book told the story of artificial intelligence (AI), starting with the ancient Greeks and finishing in about 45 years' time, in 2062.[3] It focused on the technology: on the digital machines that we are building today which will start to be as intelligent as us sometime around 2062. This book picks up where the last one ended.[4] It tells the story of where humankind will go in the century or two following the arrival of these thinking machines around 2062. It focuses not on the technology, but on us. It examines the impact that thinking machines will have on the human race.

We won't be talking about the technology of 100 or 200 years' time. As Arthur C. Clarke would have said, technology that far into the future will simply sound magical.[5] What is more important is what we *do* with this technology, for it will be the most powerful magic ever invented.

THE RISE OF *HOMO SAPIENS*

Why did we, *Homo sapiens*, become so successful? Why are we the ones who, for better or worse, dominate this planet? Why did *Homo sapiens* replace *Homo neanderthalensis*?

The Neanderthals weren't so different from us. They shared some 99.7 per cent of our DNA. They were a little shorter and stockier than us, which gave them a smaller surface-to-volume ratio and meant they were better adapted to a seasonal climate. And despite the myth about their intelligence, they actually had larger brains than us. When you adjust for our differing body sizes, the Neanderthals' brain was proportionally quite comparable to that of *Homo sapiens*.

So what gave us the edge? We may never know for sure. But one very likely candidate is language. Around 100,000 years ago, *Homo sapiens* started to develop complex spoken language. By contrast, the Neanderthals appear to have had, at best, a simple proto-language. This proto-language was probably closer to music than to speech.

It's hard to be certain that this really was the reason for our success. For most of the twentieth century, it was not considered scientifically respectable to discuss the origins of language. Given the limited evidence available at that time, much debate about the topic had been highly speculative. Many considered that the discussion of how language came into being was in fact not very useful. The Linguistics Society of Paris, when it was founded in 1866, included the following in its statutes: 'The Society accepts no communications concerning either the origin of language, or the creation of a universal language.' The London-based Philological Society installed a similar ban in 1872.

For much of the twentieth century, then, linguists mostly studied the structure of language as it exists today, and gave little consideration to how it came to be that way. But it's an important question. How was it that *Homo sapiens* alone developed complex language? And what impact did that have on our evolution?

Even in the 1970s, when it started to become respectable again to discuss the origins of language, the debate mostly stuck to the way language had evolved, rather than when it did, or how language had affected our evolution. Linguists argued about whether language was innate, as Noam Chomsky would have us believe, or whether it evolved over time from some simpler proto-language. Less attention was given to the immense impact that language appears to have had on the capacity of our species to dominate the planet.

THE IMPACT OF LANGUAGE

Before we had spoken language, our ability to learn was somewhat limited. Each generation had to relearn a lot from scratch. Of course, some knowledge and skills can be taught by demonstration. I can show you plants that are poisonous, or how to prepare a wooden spear, or how to drink water off leaves in the rainforest. But learning by demonstration can be slow and painful. One person has to physically show another everything they need to know. Inevitably, a lot of a person's knowledge dies with them.

Evolution is also a learning process, but one that's even slower and less precise than learning by demonstration. Genes that lead to behaviours which increase the survival rate of the organism are more likely to be passed on to the next generation. But such evolution can only go so far. Cows haven't evolved to farm hay. Sharks haven't evolved to farm seals. And, without language, it's almost certain they never will.

5

Language changed the game completely. When we had language, I could *describe* to you what plants you should and shouldn't eat: 'Don't eat the mushrooms with the spots. Or those attractive-looking red berries.' I can also describe to you how to catch a deer: 'Always approach from upwind and with the sun behind you. Dawn or dusk is best.' And how to farm wheat: 'Plant in the spring, and harvest at the end of summer. Wait for the frosts to end before you plant.'

But language did much more than just make it easier for the next generation to hunt food, gather crops and farm the land. It gave us stories, myths, religion. Language gave us astronomy and astrology, geography, history, economics, politics. And it gave us science, technology and medicine. It was language that put the *sapiens* in *Homo sapiens*.

Societies developed and grew stronger because of language. Language helped us work together, resolve conflicts and trust one other. Language enabled us to develop barter economies and, in time, monetary economies. Language helped people specialise in different roles. It powered education and led to the formation of our political systems.

Importantly, language meant that we learned not only individually but as a society. Our might was now *collective*. Knowledge was no longer lost so readily when someone died. It could be communicated across generations, quickly and easily.

The Neanderthals didn't stand a chance.

THE IMPACT OF WRITING

Homo sapiens took another leap forward when language became written as well as spoken. This provided a second step-change in how we came to dominate the planet.

Writing was first developed in China around 5000 BCE, and independently in Mesopotamia in around 3100 BCE. Writing enabled societies to become even more complex. Cities began to become the established centres of communal life, and writing codified the laws governing them. People were now able to record transactions and property rights, and develop a criminal code. Writing allowed cities to function in a more ordered manner.

Writing meant that learning was no longer restricted by time or space. With spoken language, you could only learn from someone within earshot, which pretty much limited you to your immediate social group. But once knowledge could be written down, you had access to a much wider group of people.

Initially, of course, writing was slow and expensive. Scribes painstakingly copied texts by hand. It would take over 100 days to copy the Bible this way, for instance. Much of the population remained illiterate, and profited only indirectly from the benefits writing brought.

A third step-change came about much more recently, with printing. Johannes Gutenberg invented the printing press around 1440 CE. In the next hundred years or so, fewer than 100,000 books were printed in the whole of Europe. During the next century, though, this tripled to over 300,000 books. And in the following hundred years, book production doubled again to nearly 700,000 books. Today, books are a billion-dollar industry, employing hundreds of thousands of people and producing millions of new titles each year.[6]

With the printing press greatly reducing the cost and time required of producing books, it was no coincidence that the period we call the Renaissance followed. Ideas and learning could now spread quickly and easily. Today, the internet lets us share information planet-wide at very little expense. Knowledge has become cheap and plentiful. And humans have become much smarter.

CO-LEARNING

The next step-change is happening right now. It's a concept I've called 'co-learning'. This is an idea closely related to – but subtly different from – the concept of collective learning.

Sociologists, anthropologists and others describe *Homo sapiens* advancing by groups learning together across generations. This is *collective learning*. Each generation learns collectively from the last. As a group we are more intelligent, but no single individual is necessarily more intelligent. Co-learning, on the other hand, is learning not by a group but by *every individual* within a group. In co-learning, every person learns everything that anyone else in the group learns. Every individual in the group shares the same knowledge, so every individual in the group becomes more intelligent.

With spoken language, co-learning can happen across groups containing tens or hundreds of people. You explain something to me, and I learn it. With written language, we can increase this to the millions or even billions. You write down something you have learned, and anyone with access to this writing can learn the same thing. But there are many skills that we cannot articulate to other people. It is just as painful for you to learn to ride a bicycle as it was for me. There's little I can say or write down that will make it any easier for you.

Nor is language the perfect medium for co-learning, as the language we communicate in is probably *not* the language of thought. We have to translate our thoughts into language, then write or speak those ideas. The other person then has to take this language and translate it back into thoughts. This is a slow, difficult and challenging process.

This brings us to the final step-change in learning – the one that will give *Homo digitalis* an unbeatable advantage. Co-learning is starting to take place not by means of language but via computer code. And computer code is a much better way to co-learn: I simply share a copy of my code with you. There is no need for translation backwards and forwards, and the code is directly and immediately executable. And unlike our memories, code doesn't decay. Once learnt, it is never forgotten. It's hard to think of a better method for co-learning than sharing computer code.

PLANET-WIDE LEARNING

Companies such as Tesla and Apple are already starting to co-learn on a global scale. Apple, for instance, is using co-learning to improve its speech-recognition software. Every Apple smartphone on the planet learns and improves the code used to recognise speech by every other Apple smartphone. Similarly, Tesla is using co-learning to improve its autonomous driving. Every Tesla car can improve its own driving and that of every other Tesla car. Each night, Tesla cars can download and share the latest improvements in their software. If one Tesla has learnt how to avoid an errant shopping trolley, every other Tesla on the planet quickly knows how to do so too.

Co-learning is one reason why *Homo sapiens* doesn't stand a chance against *Homo digitalis*. It's also one of the reasons that we're going to be surprised by the speed with which *Homo digitalis* arrives. We're used to learning everything pretty much from scratch for ourselves. We have no personal experience of learning at a planet-wide scale.

Imagine if you could co-learn like computers can, by simply sharing code. You would be able to speak every language in the world. You would be able to play chess as well as Garry Kasparov, and Go as well as Lee Sedol. You would be able to prove theorems as easily as Euler, Gauss or Erdős. You could write poetry to rival Wordsworth or Shakespeare. You would be able to play every musical instrument. All in all, your abilities would match the best abilities of anyone on the planet. And you would only ever get better at any of these activities. This might sounds scary, but it's our co-learning future when *Homo digitalis* starts sharing its computer code.

To understand fully the benefits of co-learning with computer code, you need to understand two other powerful ideas. First, that computers are *universal* machines that can run *any* program. And second, that programs can modify themselves. In particular, a program can modify itself to get better at a given task. Let me explain in some more detail why these are such powerful concepts, and why they will give *Homo digitalis* such an edge over us.

UNIVERSAL MACHINES

Alan Turing was one of the fathers of AI. He famously asked what it would mean for a computer to think. He also laid the foundations of computing itself. He came up with a simple but revolutionary idea: the *universal* computing machine. This is a machine that can compute anything that can be computed. Yes, you read me right. Ever since Turing came up with this idea, we've been able to build a computer that, in principle, can compute anything that *any* computer, even those yet to be invented, can compute.

Central to the idea of a universal computing machine are the concepts of a *program* and the *data* on which this program operates.[7] Programs are sequences of instructions that a computer follows when solving a problem. Think of them as recipes. Data is the different information that the program acts upon – analogous to the ingredients used in a particular cooking session.

Consider the problem of updating someone's bank balance when they make an electronic payment. We can write a program that will do this regardless of the payment amount or the person making the payment. The data that the program acts on is a database of customer names and their bank balances, plus the name of the customer making the payment, and the payment amount.

The program for making an electronic payment works as follows. First, the program looks up the person's name and bank balance in the database. Second, the program deducts the payment from the balance. Third, the program updates the new balance in the database. Simple – but immensely powerful. By changing the data, we can deduct payment from a different customer, or even from a database of customers of a different bank. And if we change the program, the computer can do something new. For instance, if we add the payment instead of deducting it, we have a program to make electronic deposits rather than electronic payments.

A computer, then, is an example of a *universal* machine as it can run *any* program. This is the secret of the smartphone sitting in your pocket. It can be loaded with new apps, which are programs that allow it to do tasks that the creators of the smartphone themselves have not envisaged. In this way, smartphones have become so much more than phones: they are navigators, calendars, alarm clocks, calculators, note takers, music players, games consoles and, increasingly, personal assistants.

Advances in technology might bring us faster computers, but they won't be able to compute anything more than the universal machine first dreamt about by Turing back in the 1930s. Most remarkable of all, Turing came up with this idea of a universal computing machine *before* the first computers had even been built.

What's more, computers are the *only* universal machines that humankind has invented. Think about what a universal travel machine might be. This would enable us to fly in the air, swim underwater and travel overland. It could run on rails, over tarmac, across grass, even through quicksand. It could carry one person or a dozen. Heck, it could even fly you to the moon. Think Transformers – on steroids.

To perform some new task, a computer just needs a new program. This makes computers infinitely adaptable. The computers we have now have the potential to do much more than they do today. They even have the potential to become artificially intelligent. We just need to find the right program for our computer to run.

This brings us to the next powerful idea. We don't even have to *find* that new program because the computer can actually find it for itself. It can *learn* to do new tasks. It can even learn to behave intelligently.

MACHINES THAT LEARN

How can a computer learn to do something new? After all, a computer program is just a fixed sequence of instructions, specified by some computer code. Actually, the term 'computer code' is a good one, as a program's instructions really are specified by a cryptic code. On a Z80 computer, for example, the code 87 signifies that we add two numbers together, while 76 signifies the end of the program. And on a 6800 computer, the code 8B adds numbers, while DD ends the program.[8]

The important thing about code is not that it is cryptic but that it is simply data. A sequence of numbers. This is an immensely powerful idea. If we want to change the program, we simply load some new code as data. And what is even more powerful: because a program can change its own data, a program can *change itself.* This is the heart of machine learning: the idea that a computer can learn from its data and change its own code to improve its performance over time.

It's not that important to know how machine-learning algorithms go about deciding what changes to make to their code. Some are inspired by evolution, creating mutations and crossovers of the code like the mutations and crossovers of genes in sexual reproduction. Others are inspired by the brain itself, updating links between artificial neurons like the neural reinforcement that occurs in our brains when we learn. In either case, the computer keeps the changes that improve performance and throws out those that don't. Slowly but surely, the computer learns to do better.

We already have one very good example of how to build intelligence. It's us – *Homo sapiens*. Our intelligence has largely been learnt. We are born without language. Without the ability to read or write. Without knowledge of arithmetic, or astronomy, or ancient history. But we can learn all of these, and more.

Machine learning is likely to be an important part of computers that think. It tackles the *knowledge bottleneck*, the problem of pouring into a machine all the knowledge we have developed over thousands of years. Programming all that knowledge ourselves, fact by fact, would be slow and painful. But we don't need to do this, as computers can simply learn it for themselves.

We can see now why computers can be so much better than humans at learning. They can write a program that knows how to improve its own code, and then they can share this code with other computers. Simple! And so much more effective than how we humans learn.

The next time you're trying to teach one of your children how to compute the maximum of a mathematical function or to decline a German verb, think how much easier it would be to teach her if she were a computer. You'd simply give her the code.

COMPUTERS DO MORE THAN THEY ARE TOLD

Machine learning has fuelled many of the recent spectacular advances in AI. It powered Google's AlphaGo to beat the best human Go players on the planet. It is the secret sauce behind Google Translate. And it powers many other programs that can now beat humans at tasks such as diagnosing skin cancer and playing poker.

One common reaction to the idea of machine learning is that computers will only do what you program them to do. On a simple level, this is correct. Computers are entirely deterministic.[9] They follow the instructions written in their computer code. They do not deviate – they cannot deviate. But on a deeper level, computers can do things they weren't explicitly programmed to do. They can learn new programs. They can even be creative. Just like us, they can learn to do new things from their experiences.

AlphaGo wasn't programmed to play the ancient Chinese game of Go better than a world champion. It learned by playing itself millions of times. The reason that it got better than humans was that it played more games of Go than any human could in a lifetime. And in learning to play Go well, it even became a little creative. It used moves that Go masters never expected, opening up new possibilities in how Go is played.

And AlphaGo isn't alone. Computers are now better than humans in a wide variety of games, including backgammon, poker, Scrabble and chess. When someone tells me that computers can only do what they have been programmed to do, I like to list half a dozen games where computers are already world champion. In almost every case, these computer programs were programmed by players of intermediate ability, and the program became a world champion by *learning* to play better than humans.

THE MACHINE ADVANTAGE

To understand why *Homo sapiens* is set to be replaced, you need to understand the many advantages computers have over humans – and that the digital world has over the analog. Co-learning is one important advantage, but let's look at some others.

The first is that computers can have a much more expansive memory capacity than humans. Everything we remember has to be stored in our bony craniums. Indeed, we already pay a significant price for having heads as big as they are. Until recently, childbirth was one of the major causes of death for women. And the size of the birth canal limits us from having bigger heads still. Computers have no such limits. We can simply add more storage.

The second advantage is that computers can work at much higher speeds than humans. The brain works at under 100 Hz as neurons take over 1/100th of a second each to fire. Our brains are chemical as well as electrical, which slows them down further. It takes time for chemicals to cross nerve boundaries, and for chemical reactions to take place. Computers, on the other hand, are bound only by the laws of physics. The speed of computers has gone up from 5 MHz in 1981 (that is, able to execute five instructions every millionth of a second) to around 5 GHz today (able to execute five instructions every billionth of a second). Of course, speed alone is not a very good measure today of performance. Raw computer speed has not increased much lately. Instead, computers now get faster by doing more at once. Just like the human brain, computers now execute several instructions simultaneously. Nevertheless, there remains a fundamental speed advantage of silicon over biology.

The third advantage that machines have over humans is that, unlike computers, humans have a limited power supply. Our brains use around 20 watts of the 100 watts an adult body produces.[10] The evolutionary advantage of being smart justifies investing so much of our body's limited power in the brain, but we don't have any spare power to invest in more thinking. By comparison, an average laptop can draw up to 60 watts of power. And if you want more power (or computation), you can simply run jobs in the cloud. The 7 billion human brains on the planet collectively consume around 14 gigawatts of power. By comparison, computing worldwide already uses more than ten times that amount of power. In fact, computing today accounts for 10 per cent of the world's electricity use, or over 200 gigawatts. And this number will only grow.

The fourth advantage that computers have over humans is that humans need rest and sleep. Computers can work 24/7 and never tire. As we saw earlier, AlphaGo became so good at Go because it played more games of Go than any human ever could. Of course, for humans, sleep likely serves various purposes beyond resting and recovering strength. It may help us update our memories, for instance, and tackle problems subliminally. Perhaps computers might benefit in the same way? We could choose to program them to sleep for a day every so often.

The fifth advantage that computers have over humans is that humans are forgetful, while computers aren't. Think how often you've wasted time looking for a lost object. Or forgotten a birthday. Forgetting can sometimes be useful, or course, helping us ignore irrelevant details – but it's a trivial matter to program computers to forget.

The sixth advantage is that humans can be blinded by their emotions. Computers today have no emotions and so cannot be blinded. On the other hand, emotions play an important role in our lives, and often influence our decision-making in positive ways too. It seems likely, therefore, that they have evolutionary value. We may choose to give emotions to computers in the future. In chapter three, I'll discuss this in more detail, along with other challenging topics such as consciousness.

The seventh advantage computers have over humans is one we have explored already: that humans are limited in how we can share our knowledge and skills, while computers are not. Any computer can run the code of any other computer. When one computer learns to translate from Mandarin to English, we can give that ability to every computer. When one computer learns to diagnose melanoma, we can give that skill to every computer. Computers are the ultimate co-learners.

The eight advantage is that humans are, in reality, rather poor decision-makers. We've evolved to be good enough to survive, but this is far from optimal. We're terrible at calculating exact probabilities, for instance. We would never buy lottery tickets if we were better at this. But we can program computers to be optimal. The field of behavioural economics studies our suboptimal decisions. For instance, we are often driven not to maximise our profits but to avoid losses. Behavioural economists call this *loss aversion*. There are many other examples of suboptimal behaviour. Many of us fear flying when it is the drive to the airport we should be more worried about. We know we should lose a few pounds, but that jam donut is just so tasty.

Of course, it's not all one way. Computers aren't better than us in all respects. Humans have a couple of major advantages over computers. Our brains are still more complex than even the largest supercomputers. We are quick learners, and have astounding creativity, emotional intelligence and social empathy. But I very much doubt that we will maintain these advantages over computers in the long term. We already have some evidence that computers can be creative, as well as possess emotional intelligence and empathy. In the long term, *Homo sapiens* has little hope in a race against the machines.

OUR SUCCESSOR

Who, then, is this *Homo digitalis*, this even more remarkable species that will replace us?

A species is defined by what is it and by where it acts. In the case of *Homo digitalis*, both what it is and where it acts will be increasingly digital. *Homo digitalis* will start out as the digital version of ourselves. As computers become smarter, we will out-source more and more of our thinking to them. These digital entities will no longer be held back by our complex, messy and somewhat limited brains. We will escape the limitations of bodies that need to rest and sleep, and that eventually decay and die. We will no longer be limited to observing and acting in one place at a time. We will be everywhere simultaneously.

By augmenting our brains digitally, *Homo digitalis* will be far smarter than *Homo sapiens*. Increasingly, the distinction between what we think and what is thought in the AI cloud will be hard to distinguish. *Homo digitalis* will transcend our physical self, and will be both biological and digital. We will live both in our brains and in the larger digital space.

In fact, for much of the time, *homo digitalis* will no longer have to be part of the slow, messy and dangerous analog world. Increasingly, we will live and act in a purely digital world. After a century of climate change, financial crises and terrorism, this digital world will be a welcoming, organised and well-ordered place. There will be none of the uncertainty that makes living on Earth so painful at times. There will be no earthquakes or landslides. No plagues. Everything will follow precise and fair rules. *Homo digitalis* will be the master of this digital universe. We will, in some sense, have become gods of this digital space.

That's the optimistic outcome – because we get to build this digital future. We really are gods in this sense. And we can ensure that this digital future is fair, just and beautiful. Or we can let the current forces shaping our planet define what it is, and allow it to be full of inequality, injustice and suffering. We get to choose. And we start to make these choices today.

The future is not inevitable. It is the product of the decisions we make today. But it seems likely to me that we are at a critical juncture. There are many forces pushing us towards a slippery slope, one that leads to a very troublesome and disturbing world.

We have the chance now to make some choices that will save us from this end, and guide us towards a brighter digital future. Some of these choices will be easy and cheap, others difficult and costly. They may require vision, leadership, selflessness, even sacrifice.

We have been very lucky. We've had the run of our planet – this amazing blue-green dot, revolving around a rather typical star on a minor spiral arm of the Milky Way – for the last few hundred thousand years. We owe it to our grandchildren – who will after all be of this new species *Homo digitalis* – to get the next few decades right.

WHO IS THIS BOOK FOR?

This book is written for anyone concerned about where AI is taking us. There are many issues to think about. Will AI destroy people's jobs, even those requiring creativity? Will AI become conscious? What does AI mean for the concept of free will? What ethical values will (or should) AI have? Will AI help or hurt society? Will it change how we view ourselves?

Will it change the very essence of our humanity?

You'll find my answers to these questions as I discuss the societal and ethical impacts of our shift to the digital cloud. In part, I'll examine the trends we can see today, and extrapolate from there. But the present doesn't fix the future in place. It is the choices we make now and in the near future that will determine the more distant future. I will therefore identify both the good and the not-so-good possible futures. It's up to all of us to work towards those better outcomes.

This book focuses on the year 2062. As I discuss in the next chapter, most experts in AI believe that there's a 50 per cent chance we will have created machines that can think as well as us by 2062. It's possible this date is a little optimistic and we might have to wait to around 2220 for human-level AI. Most experts believe there's a 90 per cent certainty that we will have done it by then. Whatever date it is, the magic really starts when machines surpass our own intelligence.

This book is intended for the interested but non-expert reader. There are a couple of graphs, but no equations. I don't describe what AI is, nor what is has achieved to date – for this, I refer you to my previous book *It's Alive*. In the endnotes you'll find references, additional explanations and the occasional funny observation, but you can ignore these completely and still enjoy the book.[11] However, if you do want to explore a technical idea more deeply, these notes will provide you with further details and a springboard into the literature.

The philosopher Nick Bostrom predicted in 2015 that 'in the long term, artificial intelligence will be a big deal – perhaps the most consequential thing humanity ever does'.[12] If he's right, we ought to explore those consequences.

0002

THE END OF US

We've had hundreds of years to get used to the idea that machines could be better than us. In the past, though, it was only our brawn that was outperformed, with machines that could do more physical work than any person. But in the last fifty years, it is increasingly our brains that are being overtaken – at least, if we focus on narrow intellectual tasks. By 2062 it is likely that this race will be over. *Homo digitalis* will have won.

It may come as a surprise that the first world champion was beaten by a computer nearly four decades ago. On 15 July 1979, the world backgammon champion Luigi Villa was convincingly beaten 7–1 by Hans Berliner's BKG 9.8 program. In a cruel twist, Villa had been world champion for just one day before his defeat.

More recently, it was in 1997 when the reigning world chess champion Garry Kasparov was narrowly beaten by IBM's Deep Blue computer. Describing his loss, Kasparov describes a future that awaits humankind:

> I had played a lot of computers but had never experienced anything like this. I could feel – I could smell – a new kind of intelligence across the table. While I played through the rest of the game as best I could, I was lost; it played beautiful, flawless chess the rest of the way and won easily.[1]

Like Villa's loss, Kasparov's defeat to Deep Blue was a cruel outcome. Kasparov is considered by many to be one of the greatest ever chess players. In 1985, when he first became world chess champion, he was the youngest player to reach this pinnacle of the sport. Twenty years later, when he retired from professional chess, Kasparov remained the world's highest-rated player. Sorry, he remained the highest-rated player who wasn't a computer. It is unfortunate for Kasparov that he may be remembered by some for being the first world chess champion beaten by computer.

Chess computers have progressed significantly since 1997. Neither Kasparov nor the current world champion, Magnus Carlsen, would stand a chance against the best programs available today. Indeed, Kasparov would even struggle to beat Pocket Fritz 4, which runs on a mobile phone. Pocket Fritz 4 has an Elo rating of 2898, higher than Kasparov's peak rating of 2851.[2]

When a program is given more computational resources than a mobile phone, we stand little chance at beating it. Deep Fritz, which runs on a standard PC, has an astonishing Elo rating of 3150. The 300-point difference between Kasparov and Deep Fritz means the Russian has less than a 1 in 5 chance of winning any game, and almost no chance of winning a tournament. For someone like me, with a much lower Elo rating still, there's almost no chance I could win a single game against Deep Fritz.

But human chess hasn't suffered from this machine dominance. Indeed, computer chess has improved the human game in several ways. Chess computers now provide professional coaching advice to human amateurs. And chess computers have opened up new avenues of play that we humans might never have considered. Our machine overlords have actually improved the human game.

ALL SYSTEMS ARE GO

In March 2016 another landmark in the history of AI was passed when DeepMind's AlphaGo program beat Lee Sedol, one of the best Go players on the planet. Go is an ancient and very complex Chinese board game, played by placing black or white stones on a nineteen-by-nineteen board in order to capture the most territory.

Go is significantly more challenging than chess for a variety of reasons. In chess, there might be twenty possible moves at every turn. In Go, there can be around 200 different available moves.[3] In chess, it's often not too hard to work out who is winning: every piece on the board can be given a score, and the player with the higher score is likely ahead. In Go, all the pieces are identical. Deciding who is winning requires a much more subtle consideration of what territory each player controls. It takes humans years of dedication to learn how to become good at Go.

In May 2017 DeepMind convincingly demonstrated that AlphaGo's 2016 result against Sedol was no fluke. In a $1.8-million match, an improved AlphaGo beat the Chinese Go prodigy Ke Jie, who was then ranked number one in the world.[4]

But while these two victories were landmark moments for AI, their significance has been overstated in some quarters. AlphaGo was specifically trained to play Go. It would take a lot of effort to adapt the program to play a more distant game such as poker.[5] It is doubtful that the same techniques that work in Alpha Zero (the most recent version of AlphaGo, which is designed to work from just the rules of a board game) would work in a game that incorporates chance. And certainly Alpha Zero is of no use for driving an autonomous car, writing a novel or translating a legal document.

Another misconception is that the AlphaGo result came out of the blue, and therefore points to some sort of 'exponential' improvement in AI. This is not the case. It was certainly a landmark achievement that captured people's imaginations, and DeepMind deserves every congratulation. But while AlphaGo glued together components in a new way, there wasn't anything fundamentally new about those components.[6]

The most successful computer program before AlphaGo was CrazyStone, a program written by Remi Coulom. In an interview in 2014, Coulom predicted that it would take ten years to beat a professional player. In fact, it only took AlphaGo a little over one year to beat Fan Hui, a three-time European champion, and one more to beat Lee Sedol.

However, DeepMind had thrown a lot more effort at the problem than had ever been invested before. Go programs were previously written by individuals; DeepMind had over fifty people working on AlphaGo. It took less than a tenth of the time to get there than predicted, but more than ten times the human labour was put into the problem.

DeepMind also had access to Google's vast server farms, which enabled AlphaGo to play billions and billions of games of Go against itself. If you did nothing but play Go for your whole life, you still couldn't get close to playing that many games. So AlphaGo is actually a very slow learner. In contrast to programs like this, humans can learn from single examples. We still struggle to build AI programs that can learn from so little data. So, while AlphaGo's victories were a symbolic moment for AI, it was perhaps not the step-change that Google's PR department might have led you to believe.[7]

BEYOND GAMES

Games offer a simple challenge for AI. They typically have clear rules and an obvious winner. And games like chess and Go are generally considered to require a reasonable level of intelligence of players. It's not surprising, then, that they've been a natural test-bed for AI research.

But it's not just in games like these that machines have gotten better than humans. In a number of more practical areas we are seeing computers starting to outperform humans. In medicine, computers are now better than doctors in certain respects, such as electrocardiograms. A Stanford University team led by Andrew Ng, former head of AI research at Baidu, has built a machine-learning model that can identify heart arrhythmia from an electrocardiogram better than a human expert.

Cancer provides a second example. A Google team managed to use machine learning to detect breast cancer from pathology reports more accurately than human doctors. And it does so much more quickly – and, thus, more cheaply – than humans. A third example: back in the 1980s, the expert system PUFF was diagnosing lung disease in a Californian hospital alongside human physicians. Artificial intelligence is already giving us better, faster and cheaper healthcare.

In business, there are also many areas where computers are outperforming humans. Take the stock market. BlackRock is the world's largest money manager. It is in charge of over $5 trillion of funds. Many of its actively managed funds are now run by algorithms. The computer has an edge over human fund managers due to the sheer volume of data it can analyse. Computers can do tasks that no human can do, such as monitoring satellite data of store carparks and internet searches to predict sales volume and economic growth.

Insurance is another area in which computers are taking over from humans. In Japan, Fukoku Mutual Life Insurance is now processing payouts using Watson, IBM's AI offering. When it started using Watson, it laid off thirty-four employees who had performed this task. The company now expects to save over $1 million every year.

As a third example, let's turn to the law. A number of start-ups, including Luminance, can automatically process large and unstructured datasets to help lawyers perform due diligence on contracts. The software can find anomalies in half the time it took before. It also reduces the expertise needed to complete such tasks.

Such applications of AI are already transforming many areas of work. Indeed, it's hard to think of a sector of the economy that won't be impacted by 2062.

ARTIFICIAL GENERAL INTELLIGENCE

All the AI systems we've discussed so far solve one narrow problem. Playing Go. Reading mammograms. Picking stocks. The goal of artificial *general* intelligence (AGI) is to build programs that can do *anything* as well as – if not better than – humans. We are still some distance from AGI. And, contrary to the hype you read in some of the press today, there are some substantial obstacles between where we are today and AGI.

First, humans are quick learners. We have to be. It's baked into our DNA. When you're being chased by a tiger, you don't have time to learn from many mistakes. AI systems, on the other hand, are still rather slow learners. The recent success of deep learning, in areas such as playing Go, transcribing Mandarin and recognising images, has occured on the back of a huge amount of data.

There are many settings where we don't have lots of data – indeed, there are many where we will *never* have lots of data. My robot, for example, will break if it falls over too many times while learning to walk. Similarly, we cannot have much data on your rare medical condition. Or on predicting stock market crashes. To address these vacuums, we need to build AI systems that can learn quickly, like humans do.

Second, humans are good at explaining their decisions. That's another important part of our decision-making. I might not accept the doctor's decision to operate if she can't explain why the operation is necessary. The nuclear power reactor needs to explain why it is shutting down. In contrast, AI systems today still tend to be black boxes.[8] They give answers but cannot explain how they came to those answers. A deep learning algorithm can tell you that this is a photograph of a cat. But it can't tell you why it is a cat. That it is a cat because it has fur, four legs and cute little paws. And it can't tell you why it is not a dog. We still need to build AI systems that can explain their decisions.

Third, humans have a very deep understanding of our world. When we are born, we know almost nothing about the world and how it works. That an apple falls to the ground under the pull of gravity. That rain is evaporated water falling from the sky. That the Earth goes around the Sun, and the Moon around the Earth. Indeed, that the Moon is falling under the same gravitational force that pulls the apple to the ground. We learn all these things, and many more. We bring all this information together, and synthesise it into a deep understanding of how our universe works.

But AI systems today have no such understanding. When you ask a machine to translate 'The man was pregnant', it has no understanding of why this is odd. When you show it an image of someone letting go of an apple, it has no idea that the apple will fall to the ground, accelerating at 9.8 m/s^2. We still need to develop AI systems that understand the world like we do, wholistically. Systems that have, for instance, our common sense.

Fourth, humans are very adaptable. Parachute us into a new situation and we will start to adapt and cope. When the oxygen tank on Apollo 13 exploded, the world held its breath for three days while the astronauts and flight controllers adapted to the seemingly impossible and returned the astronauts safely to Earth. This adaptability has helped us become the dominant species both on and, in this case, off the planet.

AI systems, on the other hand, are immensely brittle. Change the problem even in a small way and they tend to break. And not gracefully. In fact, there's a subfield of AI devoted to finding ways to break AI systems. What is the smallest change to an image that stops the algorithm from recognising the stop sign? What is the most different image that the algorithm incorrectly 'recognises'? We are still yet to build AI systems that degrade gracefully, as human performance does.

HOW LONG HAVE WE GOT?

In a number of narrow domains, machines have surpassed human performance. But we have a long distance to go before we can build AGI. When will we get there? And how long will it then take for computers to become much smarter than us? Is this going to be our problem? Or our children's or grandchildren's problem? Given the millions of years it took for human intelligence to evolve, perhaps it is even farther away? Might it take many centuries, or even millennia? Or might it never happen?

At a 2017 conference in Asilomar on the future of AI, Andrew McAfee observed: 'Anyone making confident predictions about anything having to do with the future of Artificial Intelligence is either kidding you or kidding themselves.' I shall ignore this wise advice and try to make some confident predictions. Actually, I won't make the predictions: I'll get a load of AI experts to make them. Let's hope there is wisdom in this crowd.

In January 2017, I asked over 300 of my colleagues, all researchers working in AI, to give their best estimate of the time it will take to overcome the obstacles to AGI. And to put their answers in perspective, I also asked nearly 500 non-experts for their opinion.

The non-experts were readers of a news article I wrote about the AI poker program Libratus, which had just beaten some top human players. At the end of my article, I asked readers to complete a small survey on man versus machine. I was expecting there might be some mismatch between the predictions of the experts and the non-experts. I was right.

Given that there's a lot of uncertainty about how long it might take to build human-level intelligence in a machine, the survey asked both the experts and the non-experts for three predictions. When will there be a 10 per cent probability that a computer can carry out most human professions at least as well as a typical human? And when will there be a 50 per cent probability? And a 90 per cent probability? This repeats questions asked in an earlier 2012 study, reported in Nick Bostrom's book *Superintelligence*.

With advances in AI having attracted a lot of publicity in recent years, I was interested to see if the dates people nominated might be closer than they were in 2012. Bostrom's survey was one of the main pieces of evidence for his argument that AI poses a relatively imminent existential threat to humankind. If the arrival of AGI is expected sooner, we may need to take his warnings even more seriously.

But this was not the case. Experts in my survey were significantly more cautious than the non-experts about the challenges of building human-level intelligence. For a 90 per cent probability that computers match humans, the median prediction of the experts was 2112, compared to just 2060 among the non-experts.[9]

Hollywood and the current hype around AI may explain the half-century of difference. I often joke that the best thing AI could do to improve its public perception, and to quieten down people's fears, would be to start a script office in Los Angeles.

For a 50 per cent probability, the median prediction of the experts was 2062. That's where the title of this book comes from: the year in which, on average, my colleagues in AI expect humankind to have built machines that are as capable as humans. This compares to a prediction by the non-experts of 2039, over two decades earlier. The non-experts were a little more optimistic than Ray Kurzweil, futurist and director of engineering at Google, who predicts that computer will surpass humans around 2045.

Finally, for a 10 per cent probability of computers matching humans, the median prediction of the experts was 2034. The non-experts, on the other hand, predicted just 2026. That's in less than a decade. It's roughly twice as soon as the experts predict.

Why are experts less optimistic than non-experts? One of the perception problems surrounding AI is that people see systems playing complex games such as chess and Go and, reasoning that these games require lots of intelligence, imbue these systems with all the other intellectual abilities that we humans have. In the case of human chess and Go players, this is a reasonable assumption. A good Go player is likely to be an intelligent person. But that's not the case with computers. A good Go program isn't necessarily even able to play chess. And there's a very long distance between playing Go and doing many of the other tasks humans can do that require intelligence.

My view, and that of the majority of my colleagues in AI, is that it'll be at least half a century before we see computers matching humans. Given that various breakthroughs are needed, and it's very hard to predict when breakthroughs will happen, it might even be a century or more. If that's the case, you don't need to lose too much sleep tonight.

THE TECHNOLOGICAL SINGULARITY

One reason for believing that machines will get to human-level or even superhuman-level intelligence quickly is the dangerously seductive idea of the technological singularity. This idea can be traced back to a number of people over fifty years ago: John von Neumann, one of the fathers of computing, and the mathematician and Bletchley Park cryptographer I.J. Good. More recently, it's an idea that has been popularised by the science-fiction author Vernor Vinge and the futurist Ray Kurzweil.

The singularity is the anticipated point in humankind's history when we have developed a machine so intelligent that it can recursively redesign itself to be even more intelligent. This new machine would then be able to redesign itself to be even more intelligent. The idea is that this would be a tipping point, and machine intelligence would suddenly start to improve exponentially, quickly exceeding human intelligence by orders of magnitude.

Once we reach the technological singularity, we will no longer be the most intelligent species on the planet. It will certainly be an interesting moment in our history. One fear is that it will happen so quickly that we won't have time to monitor and control the development of this super-intelligence, and that this super-intelligence might lead – intentionally or unintentionally – to the end of the human race.

Proponents of the technological singularity – who, tellingly, are usually not AI researchers but futurists or philosophers – behave as if the singularity is inevitable. To them, it is a logical certainty; the only question mark is when. However, like many other AI researchers, I have considerable doubt about its inevitability.

We have learned, over half a century of work, how difficult it is to build computer systems with even modest intelligence. And we have never built a single computer system that can recursively self-improve. Indeed, even the most intelligent system we know of on the planet – the human brain – has made only modest improvements in its cognitive abilities. It is, for example, still as painfully slow today for most of us to learn a second language as it always was. Little of our understanding of the human brain has made the task easier. Since 1930, there has been a significant and gradual increase in intelligence test scores in many parts of the world. This is called the Flynn effect, after the New Zealand researcher James Flynn, who has done much to identify the phenomenon. However, explanations for this have tended to focus on improvements in nutrition, healthcare and access to school, rather than on how we educate our young people.[10]

There are multiple technical reasons why the technological singularity might never happen. I discussed many of these in my last book. Nevertheless, the meme that the singularity is inevitable doesn't seem to be getting any less popular. Given the importance of the topic – it may decide the fate of the human race – I will return again to these arguments, in greater detail, and in light of recent developments in the debates. I will also introduce some new arguments against the inevitability of the technological singularity.

FASTER-THINKING DOGS

My first objection to the supposed inevitability of the singularity is an idea that has been called the *faster-thinking dog* argument. Its considers the consequences of being able to think faster. While computer speeds may have plateaued, computers nonetheless still process data faster and faster. They achieve this by exploiting more and more parallelism, doing multiple tasks at the same time, a little like the brain.

There's an expectation that by being able to think longer and harder about problems, machines will eventually become smarter than us. And we certainly have benefited from ever-increasing computer power; the smartphone in your pocket is evidence of that. But processing speed alone probably won't get us to the singularity.

Suppose that you could increase the speed of the brain of your dog. Such a faster-thinking dog would still not be able to talk to you, play chess or compose a sonnet. For one thing, it doesn't possess complex language. A faster-thinking dog will likely still be a dog. It will still dream of chasing squirrels and sticks. It may think these thoughts more quickly, but they will likely not be much deeper. Similarly, faster computers alone will not yield higher intelligence.

Intelligence is a product of many things. It takes us years of experience to train our intuitions. And during those years of learning we also refine our ability to abstract: to take ideas from old situations and apply them to new, novel situations. We add to our commonsense knowledge, which helps us adapt to new circumstances. Our intelligence is thus much more than thinking faster about a problem.

THE TIPPING POINT

My second argument against the inevitability of the technological singularity is *anthropocentricity*. Proponents of the singularity place a special importance on human intelligence. Surpassing human intelligence, they argue, is a tipping point. Computers will then recursively be able to redesign and improve themselves. But why is human intelligence such a special point to pass?

Human intelligence cannot be measured on some single, linear scale. And even if it could be, human intelligence would not be a single point, but a spectrum of different intelligences. In a room full of people, some people are smarter than others. So what metric of human intelligence are computers supposed to pass? That of the smartest person in the room? The smartest person on the planet today? The smartest person who ever lived? The smartest person who might ever live in the future? The idea of passing 'human intelligence' is already starting to sound a bit shaky.

But let's put these objections aside for a second. Why is human intelligence, whatever it is, the *tipping point* to pass, after which machine intelligence will inevitably snowball? The assumption appears to be that if we are smart enough to build a machine smarter than us, then this smarter machine must also be smart enough to build an even smarter machine. And so on. But there is no logical reason that this would be the case. We might be able to build a smarter machine than ourselves. But that smarter machine might not necessarily be able to improve on itself.

There could be some level of intelligence that is a tipping point. But it could be any level of intelligence. It seems unlikely that the tipping point is *less* than human intelligence. If it were less than human intelligence, we humans could likely simulate such a machine today, use this simulation to build a smarter machine, and thereby already start the process of recursive self-improvement.

So it seems that any tipping point is at, *or* above, the level of human intelligence. Indeed, it could be well above human intelligence. But if we need to build machines with much greater intelligence than our own, this throws up the possibility that we might not be smart enough to build such machines.

BEYOND INTELLIGENCE

My third argument against the inevitability of the technological singularity concerns *meta-intelligence*. Intelligence, as I said before, encompasses many different abilities. It includes the ability both to perceive the world and to reason about that perceived world. But it also includes many other abilities, such as creativity.

The argument for the inevitability of the singularity confuses two different abilities. It conflates the ability to do a task and the ability to improve your ability to do a task. We can build intelligent machines that improve their ability to do particular tasks, and do these tasks better than humans. Baidu, for instance, has built Deep Speech 2, a machine-learning algorithm that learned to transcribe Mandarin better than humans. But Deep Speech 2 has not improved our ability to learn tasks. It takes Deep Speech 2 just as long now to learn to transcribe Mandarin as it always has. Its superhuman ability to transcribe Mandarin hasn't fed back into improvements of the basic deep-learning algorithm itself. Unlike humans, who get to be better learners as they learn new tasks, Deep Speech 2 doesn't learn faster as it learns more.

Improvements to deep-learning algorithms have come about the old-fashioned way: by humans thinking long and hard about the problem. We have not yet built any self-improving machines. It's not certain that we ever will.

DIMINISHING RETURNS

My fourth argument against the inevitability of the technological singularity is the curse of *diminishing returns*. Even if machines are able to improve themselves recursively, we may not be rewarded with extensive gains. We have seen diminishing returns in many other areas of human endeavour. For instance, we have repeatedly improved fuel efficiency in cars, but improvements are now becoming smaller and smaller as cars get more and more efficient.

Suppose, as an example, that we start out with a machine with average human-level intelligence. By definition, that would mean it has an IQ of 100. And suppose that, as increasing intelligence gets harder and harder, each generation of intelligent machine has an IQ that increases by 50 per cent of what it did in the previous generation. IQ is an imperfect measure of intelligence, but bear with me. The second generation of such machines would have an IQ of 150 – pretty impressive. But perhaps not as smart even as you. The third generation would have an IQ of 175, the fourth of 187.5, and so on. At no point, no matter how many generations in the future we go, can the IQ of these recursively improving machines exceed 200.

Even if we up the ante, we might still run into similar limits. Suppose each generation increased by not 50 per cent but by a more impressive 90 per cent of the last. The second generation would have an IQ of 190. The third generation would have an IQ of 271. We're now reaching the limit of documented human intelligence. The fourth generation would take us past human intelligence, to an IQ of 343.9. But no matter how many generations into the future we look, the IQ of these more impressively improving machines will never exceed 1000. They'll be very, very smart, for sure, but it's not runaway growth.

THE LIMITS OF INTELLIGENCE

My fifth argument against the inevitability of the technological singularity is the *limits of intelligence*. Even if machines are able to improve themselves recursively, we may run into fundamental limits. Many other fields have limits; why should intelligence be any different?

Science is full of limits. In physics, you cannot accelerate past the speed of light. In chemistry, there are limits to the speed of a chemical reaction. In biology, there appear to be some fundamental limits extending human life much beyond 120 years. Or running a marathon in much under two hours. Perhaps AI will also run into some fundamental limits?

If you walk into a casino and start playing roulette, it doesn't matter how smart you are, you won't beat the house. The roulette wheel is literally loaded against you. You can't be more intelligent than the person who decides to walk out of the casino. Computers can calculate probabilities much better than humans. They can thus act much more rationally than humans. But calculating probabilities to more digits of precision may not help you beat nature. The best decision might be one that even a simple and less precise calculation will reveal.

COMPUTATIONAL COMPLEXITY

My sixth argument against the inevitability of the technological singularity comes from *computational complexity*, the well-developed mathematical theory that describes the difficulty of solving different computational problems. Unless we move to machines based on forms of computation that we don't yet have today, even exponential improvements may not help due to the fundamental limits of what computers can do.

Moore's law – the doubling in computing power witnessed every two years or so – may have lulled many of us into thinking that technological progress will solve most computational challenges.[11] We live in exponential times, and exponential improvement in computing power would seem to promise that we just need to wait for enough machine generations. In ten years, computers will be over a thousand times more powerful than they are today. In twenty years, over a million. In thirty, over a billion. Surely at some point we will have enough computing power to do whatever we like? Unfortunately, this is far from being true.

Computer scientists have developed a rich theory of computational complexity. This describes how much computation is required to solve different problems in a precise and abstract way. The theory of computational complexity abstracts away the precise computer being used. It doesn't matter if it is a PC or a Mac, a smartphone or a smartwatch. A different device might change the runtime – the time it takes to solve a problem – but only by a constant factor. The game we're playing is interested in changes in runtime that are much, much bigger than mere constant factors. We may be looking for exponential increases and, as we shall see, even greater than exponential increases.

Suppose you want to compute the largest number in a list. This is a linear time problem. You have to scan through the whole list. This takes a time proportional to the size of the input, the list of numbers. If you double the size of the list, it takes twice as long to find the largest number. If you triple the size of the list, it takes three times as long to find the largest number.

Now consider how we might sort the list into order, from smallest to largest. A simple method is to find the smallest item first; as we just saw, this takes time that is proportional to the length of the list. Then you find the second-smallest item, and so on. In total, the amount of time we have to spend to sort this or indeed any list increases as the square of the length of the list. If you double the length of the list, it takes four times as long. If you triple the length of the list, it takes nine times as long. If you quadruple the length of the list, it takes sixteen times as long. This doesn't sound good. But computations can scale much, much worse than this.

There are computational problems where the runtime grows

exponentially with the size of the input. Consider a problem facing a divorcing couple of dividing their goods into two subsets, in which each subset has the same value. A simple method to find a division into equal valued subsets is to compute the sum of every possible subset of items. If any such subset has a value equal to half the total value, you have found a division into two subsets with the same value. Every time the input – a list of items – gets one item longer, the number of subsets to be considered doubles, and (in the worst case) the runtime of our algorithm doubles.

The good news is that an exponential improvement in computing power will help you solve such problems. Every doubling in your computing power will allow you to solve problems with one more item in them. Whatever the size of input you want to process, eventually it will come into range. If you need to process lists containing ten more items than is possible today, you just need to wait ten more machine generations.

But there are also computational problems where the runtime grows faster than this. An exponential improvement in computing power will then be inadequate to solve bigger problems. Consider the problem of computing the area of the Mandelbrot set. The Mandelbrot set is that beautiful fractal figure that contains amazing spirals and seahorses. It has been called the most complex figure in mathematics.

We know the Mandelbrot set has a finite area. It sits within a circle of radius 2, so its area is certainly less than 4π (=12.566 ...). But to calculate the precise area is, as far as we know, very computationally challenging. The best method we have to compute the area converges very slowly. You have to sum 10^{118} terms to get the area to within two digits of accuracy, and 10^{1181} terms to get three digits. 10^{118} is way more than the number of atoms in the universe. Exponential improvement will likely be insufficient to help with such a challenging computational problem.

FEEDBACK LOOPS

My seventh argument against the inevitability of the technological singularity comes from the fact that other undesirable feedbacks may set in, which prevent the singularity from occurring. These feedback loops may be economic or environmental.

Martin Ford gives one such argument, based on an economic feedback.[12] Before the singularity occurs, computers would be sufficiently capable that the majority of jobs in the economy would be automated. But this would cause massive unemployment. And without radical reforms to capitalism, such unemployment would cause consumer demand to collapse. This in turn would destroy the economy, preventing the investment into the research and development required to bring about the singularity.

The feedback might also be environmental. Jared Diamond has argued that societies tend to self-limit, if not collapse.[13] Their success quickly leads them to exceed the carrying capacity of their environment. Collapse follows shortly after success. In the case of AI, the increasing wealth and prosperity that it brings may stretch

48

our environment's ability to support human society. As a consequence, the technological singularity might fail to come about, simply because society collapses under an excess of consumption.

BRAKES ON INTELLIGENCE

My eighth argument against the inevitability of the technological singularity comes from Paul Allen, the co-founder of Microsoft. This is what he called the 'complexity brake'. The more progress we make towards understanding intelligence, the more difficult it becomes to make additional progress. We require more and more specialised knowledge, and we are forced to develop more and more complex scientific theories. Such a complexity brake slows down progress, preventing any runaway in machine intelligence. Allen writes:

> The amazing intricacy of human cognition should serve as a caution to those who claim the singularity is close. Without having a scientifically deep understanding of cognition, we can't create the software that could spark the singularity. Rather than the ever-accelerating advancement predicted by Kurzweil, we believe that progress toward this understanding is fundamentally slowed by the complexity brake.[14]

Allen observes that we will not get to machine intelligence just by developing faster computer hardware. We will also need significant improvements in software. And such improvements will likely require us to make breakthroughs in our understanding of human cognition. This is where the complexity brake kicks in. Human cognition looks a very difficult nut to crack.

EXTRAPOLATE WITH CARE

My ninth argument against the inevitability of the technological singularity is that we should be very wary of people extrapolating from graphs – especially graphs with logarithmic axes. *The Economist* demonstrated this with an amusing example: the humble disposable razor.[15] You may not have noticed but razor blades have been increasing exponentially in number. Let me prove it with a simple graph.

MOORE'S LAW FOR RAZORS?

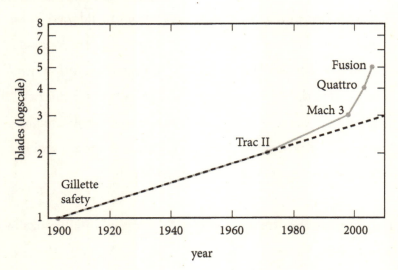

THE END OF US

The tried and tested method of demonstrating exponential growth is to plot a graph with a logarithmic vertical scale: 1, 2, 4, 8, and so on. On such a compressed scale, exponential growth becomes a simple straight line.

The dashed line in the graph represents exponential growth in the number of blades on a disposable razor. It's what you get if the number of blades doubled every sixty-eight years. In reality, you can see the number of blades has grown much faster than exponential. One blade in 1903. Two blades sixty-eight years later, in 1971. Another doubling to four blades just thirty-two years later, in 2003. Extrapolating from the first 100 years of disposable razor technology, you would expect to have only two-bladed razors now – not the five we actually have. So there has been a Moore's law for razors. But don't expect a shaving singularity anytime soon.

You might complain that I tricked you by using small numbers. It wasn't hard to get exponential growth when we only went from the single-bladed Gillette safety razor in 1903 to the five-bladed Fusion in 2006. So let me give you an example where the numbers aren't small.

Consider the number of Uber drivers on the planet. Uber calls them 'driver-partners' but, as we discuss shortly, they're anything but partners in the business. Again, to demonstrate exponential growth, I will plot a graph with a logarithmic scale that compresses the vertical axis. Every tick on the vertical axis represents a doubling of the number of Uber drivers: 5000; 10,000; 20,000; 40,000; 80,000; 160,000; and so on.

MOORE'S LAW FOR UBER?

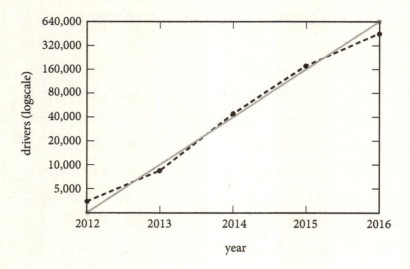

Here too the dashed line indicates exponential growth. We see again that there has been a Moore's law in the number of Uber drivers. Every year since the business started, the number of Uber drivers has roughly quadrupled. There were 8500 drivers in 2013. A more than fourfold increase to 45,000 drivers in 2014. And a fourfold increase again to 180,000 drivers in 2015.[16] But that doesn't mean we will have some sort of Uber singularity, where everyone on the planet is driving for Uber. Ultimately, this exponential increase is unsustainable. The number of Uber drivers must plateau at some point. We will hit market saturation.

A simple 'viral' model explains why, at least initially, the number of Uber drivers might be expected to quadruple every year. Suppose that, every six months, each Uber driver encourages one friend to start driving for Uber. The company probably offers them a bonus when they do. This is precisely what you need to stimulate such exponential growth.

Suppose Uber starts with 10,000 drivers at the beginning of the first year. Then these 10,000 drivers introduce 10,000 new drivers in the first six months. This gives 20,000 drivers in total. These 20,000 drivers introduce another 20,000 new drivers in the next six months. As a result, by the start of the second year, Uber has 40,000 drivers. In a similar way, at the start of the third year Uber will have 160,000 drivers; and 640,000 drivers at the start of the fourth year. (These are pretty much the numbers that happened.)

Like any pyramid scheme, such exponential growth must eventually stop. Uber drivers run out of friends who aren't already Uber drivers. Uber runs out of demand for more Uber drivers. Other rival taxi companies start offering more attractive working conditions than Uber – and that's not going to be too hard ... Anyway, for many reasons the pyramid collapses.

There are, it seems, many sets of statistics we can measure that look exponential for a while: the number of blades in a disposable razor, the number of Uber drivers, even the average cost of higher education. But that doesn't mean they will reach some sort of singularity. There are lots of laws, of both physics and economics, that prevent exponential patterns from continuing.

LEARNING FROM THE PAST

This brings me to my tenth and final argument against the inevitability of the technological singularity. We must learn from the mistakes of past historians. In fact, we must learn from the past mistakes of one of the very first singularitarians.

Henry Adams was one of the first people to write about the idea of the technological singularity. He was a grandson of John Quincy Adams, the sixth president of the United States, and a great-grandson of John Adams, the second president and one of the Founding Fathers. In 1904 Henry Adams published an autobiography, *The Education of Henry Adams*, that looked at the dawning twentieth century from the perspective of his youth, fifty years before. The book won the Pulitzer Prize and is included on the list of the 100 most important nonfiction books of the twentieth century.

Chapter 34, 'The Law of Acceleration', proposes 'a law of acceleration, definite and constant as any law of mechanics, [which] cannot be supposed to relax its energy to suit the convenience of man'. Based on this law, Adams argued that scientific and other knowledge would expand so rapidly that society in the year 2000 would be unimaginable to people from 1900. To illustrate the law, Adams noted that every ten years between 1840 and 1900, the amount of energy released per tonne of coal had doubled. And so, he predicted, 'every American who lived into the year 2000 would know how to control unlimited power'. If only it were so!

Of course, Adams was wrong. We didn't have unlimited power in 2000. And the year 2000 wasn't quite unimaginable to the people of 1900; many in fact predicted quite well what life would look like. H.G. Wells, for example, predicted the invention of exotic new technologies like lasers and nuclear weapons.[17] And many of the trends we see today, such as industrialisation and globalisation, were already clearly visible back in 1900.

SUPER-INTELLIGENT MACHINES

The ten reasons I have given for why the technological singularity might not happen do not prove it *could* not happen. It remains a possibility. But I hope I've convinced you that it is not an inevitability. Like many of my colleagues who have tried to build machines that act a little intelligently, I am doubtful we will build machines that can recursively improve themselves anytime soon. And in that case, the technological singularity will continue to remain an interesting but fictional idea.

While I remain sceptical of the technological singularity, this doesn't mean we won't get to human-level or even superhuman-level intelligence in machines. I do think we'll get to this point. Indeed, I've spent all my adult life working towards this goal. There's nothing very special about our intelligence, nor about our biology. And for this reason I believe we will one day create machines that think. They may think in different ways to us.[18] But they will likely get to be as intelligent as us. And if machines get to human-level intelligence, it's hard to think of reasons why, ultimately, they won't surpass us. They have already done so in a number of narrow domains. Plus machines have a number of inherent advantages over humans.

But I don't imagine we will get to super-intelligence simply by sitting back and watching the machines improve themselves. I suspect we'll get to super-intelligence like we got to all the other technological advances in our lives: through hard work, through developing the science through our own ingenuity, and through painfully engineering the machines to be smarter than us.

AlphaGo learned to play Go better than any human. But AlphaGo didn't improve how it learned along the way. If you asked AlphaGo to play Go on a beginner's nine-by-nine board instead of the usual nineteen-by-nineteen board, it would have to learn again, almost from scratch. We don't know yet how to transfer what it learned on the larger board to the simpler board. A human Go player, on the other hand, could competently start playing on a nine-by-nine board instantly.

AI has a long way to go before we get to human-level intelligence, let alone super-intelligence. But I do believe we will get there. We will invent machines that are superior to us. They will be stronger, faster and more intelligent than us. But rather than replace us, I am hopeful that we'll work out how these machines can augment and extend us.

EXISTENTIAL THREATS

Hollywood has primed us to worry that evil robots will try to take over the world. Indeed, according to the movie, the Terminator will first boot up in 2029, so we therefore have maybe a dozen or so years left. Was Stephen Hawking right to suggest that super-intelligence is our greatest existential threat? At the moment we are the most intelligent species on the planet, and all other life depends on our goodwill for its continued existence. Won't our fate in turn depend on the goodwill of these superior, super-intelligent machines? Let's turn next to the question of whether super-intelligent machines might simply eliminate us. Will they mark the end of humankind?

In the movies, the machines are usually depicted as evil. But incompetence rather than malevolence seems the more likely risk. Of course we have to consider the possibility that super-intelligent machines might *unintentionally* end the human race. And there are multiple scenarios in which this might occur.

THE MIDAS TOUCH

The first risk scenario is that the goals of a super-intelligent machine may be poorly designed. This is illustrated by the Greek myth of King Midas, who was granted his wish that everything he touched would turn to gold. But the king had poorly specified what he really wanted: he didn't want his food or his daughter turned to gold.

It could be argued that AI has already witnessed this in some small and not very dangerous ways. For instance, researchers reported an experiment in 2017 in which they taught a computer to play *Coast Runners*, a boat-racing video game. Rather than complete the race course, the AI learnt to go around in small circles, crashing into other boats because this increased the score more quickly than actually finishing the race.

As they are so smart, super-intelligent machines may surprise us in the way they achieve their goals. Suppose we ask a super-intelligent machine to cure cancer. One way to do this might be to eliminate all hosts that might house cancer – bringing an end, then, to the human race. Not really quite what we wanted when we asked it to cure cancer.

Such examples suppose a rather dim view of super-intelligence. If I gave you the task of curing cancer and you started to kill people, I would probably decide you weren't that intelligent. We suppose intelligent people have learned good values and are wise to the plight of others, especially those with sentience and feelings. Shouldn't a super-intelligence be suitably *wise* as well as intelligent?

PAPERCLIPS EVERYWHERE

A second risk scenario is that even if the goals are properly specified, there may be undesirable side effects that hurt humanity. Anyone who has debugged some computer code knows how frustratingly literal computers are when they interpret instructions.

This risk is explored in a well-known thought experiment proposed by Nick Bostrom.

Suppose we build a super-intelligent machine and give it the goal to build as many paperclips as possible. Because the machine is super-intelligent, it would be very good at making paperclips. The machine might start building more and more paperclip factories. Eventually the whole planet would be turned into factories for building paperclips. The machine is doing precisely what it was asked to do, but the outcome is undesirable for humankind.

Now, Bostrom doesn't actually believe we'd give a super-intelligence the goal of maximising paperclips, especially as we realise the risks of this particular goal. Paperclip production was just chosen to demonstrate that even a mundane, arbitrary and apparently harmless goal could go seriously astray.

Like the Midas argument, this supposes a rather poor view of super-intelligence. Shouldn't a super-intelligence also be able to understand the implicit goals that are not explicitly specified? Yes, do make lots of paperclips, but not at the expense of the environment. And certainly not at the expense of the human race.

THEM OR US?

A third risk scenario is that any super-intelligence will have sub-goals that may conflict with humanity's continued existence. Suppose the super-intelligence has some overall goal, such as increasing human happiness or protecting the planet. Almost any goal like this that you can imagine will require the super-intelligence to develop the resources to carry out its actions. They will also require that the super-intelligence be allowed to continue to operate so it can achieve its goal.

But humans might turn the machine off. In addition, humans will consume resources that might be better used to achieve the super-intelligence's own goals. The logical conclusion, then, is that the super-intelligence would want us eliminated. We would not then be able to turn it off, or to consume resources which might be better used for its goals.

These sub-goals of self-preservation and the acquisition of resources have been called two of the 'basic AI drives' by Stephen Omohundro.[19] Such drives are the basic sub-goals that any sufficiently intelligent AI system is likely to have. The HAL 9000 computer in Arthur C. Clarke's *2001: A Space Odyssey* represents perhaps the best-known vision of the AI drive for self-preservation. HAL starts to kill the astronauts on board the Discovery One spacecraft in a desperate attempt to prevent them from switching the computer off.

Other basic AI drives are for improvement and creativity. AI systems will tend to become more efficient, both physically and computationally, as this will help them achieve whatever other goals they might have. And, less predictably, AI systems will tend to be creative, looking for new ways to achieve their goals more efficiently and effectively.

Efficiency isn't a bad thing; it will help us conserve our planet's limited resources. But creativity is more of a challenge. It means that super-intelligent machines will be unpredictable. They will achieve their goals in ways that we might not predict. This risk is discussed in more detail in the next section.

MOVING TARGET

A fourth risk scenario is that any super-intelligence could modify itself, start working differently, even assign itself new goals. This is especially likely if we give it the goal of making itself more intelligent. How can we be sure that the redesigned super-intelligence remains aligned with our human values? Some harmless aspect of the original system might be amplified in the new, and could be very harmful to us.

The moving target might not be just the super-intelligence, but also the bigger system in which it operates. We see this phenomenon in our human institutions: it goes under the name of 'mission creep'. You decide to send some military advisers into Vietnam, and a decade later you have hundreds of thousands of soldiers on the ground, fighting a full-scale war that cannot be won.

In a modest and not-too-harmful way, this moving target problem has already been observed in the context of AI. In 2008, Google launched Google Flu Trends. It became the poster child for using big data for social good, predicting more effectively than previous methods the timing of the influenza season around the world. Google Flu Trends used Google Search queries to predict when and where flu was becoming prevalent. If lots of people in a particular region start to ask Google 'how to treat a sore throat?' and 'what is a fever?' then perhaps flu is starting to spread. But in 2013 Google Flu Trends simply stopped working. It has now been rather quietly dropped from Google's offerings. What went wrong?

The problem was that Google Search (and the human eco-system in which it sits) is a moving target. Google Search has got better and better. And part of that improvement has been that Google suggests queries before the user has even finished typing them. These improvements appear to have introduced biases into how people use Google Search, and in turn these have damaged the ability of Google Flu Trends to work. By making Google Search better, we made flu epidemics more difficult to predict.

INDIFFERENCE

A fifth risk scenario is that any super-intelligence might simply be indifferent to our fate, just as I am indifferent to the fate of certain less intelligent life forms. If I am building a new factory, I might not particularly worry about destroying an ant colony that's in the way. I don't go out of my way to destroy the ants, but they just happen to be where my factory needs to go. Similarly, a super-intelligence might not be greatly concerned about our existence. If we happen to be in the way of its goals, we might simply be eliminated. The super-intelligence has no malevolence towards us; we are collateral damage.

The danger of an indifferent super-intelligence supposes that the super-intelligence is not dependent on humanity. We can destroy the ant colony without concern because its destruction is unlikely to bring any great side effects. But destroying humanity might have some serious side effects that a super-intelligence would want to avoid. Who is providing the infrastructure that the super-intelligence is using? The servers running in the cloud? The electricity powering the cloud? The internet connecting the cloud together? If humans are still involved in any of these services, the super-intelligence should not be indifferent to our fate.

Equally, the danger of an indifferent super-intelligence supposes that the super-intelligence might not be paternalistic towards us. In fact, I'm not sure 'paternalistic' is the right adjective here. Because of their immense intelligence, we would be like children that they might wish to protect. But we would also be their parents, whom they might wish to protect in gratitude for bringing them into existence. Both are reasons for a super-intelligence not to be indifferent to our fate.

SHOULD WE WORRY?

These existential risks depend in part on super-intelligence emerging very rapidly. If this happens, we will have little or no opportunity to see the problems coming and to correct them. But, as we have seen, there are many reasons to suppose there will not be a technological singularity. If this is the case, super-intelligence is more likely to emerge slowly, as we painstakingly build better and better systems. Most of my colleagues believe super-intelligence will take many decades, if not centuries, to arrive; if they're right, we should have plenty of time to take precautions.

You may also be relieved to know that a research community focused on AI safety has formed over the last decade. Funded in part by $10 million of grants from Elon Musk, there are now research groups in the United States, the United Kingdom and elsewhere looking for technical solutions to the sort of risks I just outlined. I am reasonably confident, in light of these efforts, that AI won't eliminate humankind anytime soon.

We cannot however completely discount the existential threat that super-intelligence poses. But we probably should focus our attention on more immediate existential threats, as well as the more immediate threats posed by AI that are not existential. And you don't need to take my word that AI is likely not to be the greatest existential risk facing humankind. A survey of fifty Nobel laureates conducted in September 2017 by *Times Higher Education* ranked the climate, population rise, nuclear war, disease, selfishness, ignorance, terrorism, fundamentalism and Donald Trump as bigger threats to humanity than AI.

PASCAL'S WAGER

Let's suppose for a moment that super-intelligence does come into existence. Even if this is a century or more away, people such as Elon Musk and Nick Bostrom have warned that we ought to be very concerned. Indeed, they fear that AI will be humankind's greatest existential threat, more pressing than nuclear annihilation, global warming and all the other dangers facing the planet today. Their fear is that the machines will get away from us, and might intentionally or unintentionally eliminate humankind.

In my view, these voices are being seduced by the classic philosophical argument devised by Blaise Pascal. Pascal was a French philosopher, mathematician and physicist who lived from 1623 to 1662. In his posthumously published *Pensées* ('Thoughts'), he put forward an argument about the necessity of believing in God that has become known as Pascal's wager.

Pascal's wager goes as follows. God exists or God doesn't exist, and you need to decide which is the case. Indeed, you must bet your life on whether God exists or not. This is the wager. It is not optional: if you do nothing, you are still taking one side of the wager.

If you believe in God and God does indeed exist, then you gain an eternal life of infinite happiness. If you believe in God and God does not exist, then your loss is finite: the actions in your finite life are governed by your belief in a God who does not exist. On the other hand, if you do not believe in God and God does exist, then your loss is infinite: you give up an eternal life of happiness. And if you do not believe in God and God does not exist, then your gain was only finite: you were spared the futile actions of a believer.

Pascal's reasoning was one of the first examples of 'decision theory', the logical theory of making the best decisions. (Today, AI is at the forefront of implementing decision theory in computers.

It's perhaps ironic, then, that the very same theoretical ideas are distracting people from the real existential threats to the planet.)

Decision theory tells us that the act of believing in God dominates the act of not believing. You can risk a finite amount in order to potentially gain an infinite amount. This is the sort of bet any banker or gambler should take without hesitation. Pascal's wager would have you logically believe in God as this maximises the potential return you can expect to get.

But logic and probability alone cannot decide whether we should believe in God. People concerned about super-intelligence are falling victim to a similar trap. The argument is as follows. The extinction of humankind might remove all life from the universe, leaving it a dead and lifeless place. It would deny the billions, perhaps trillions, of humans who would have followed us the opportunity for happiness. Indeed many proponents of the technological singularity are transhumanists who also believe we'll conquer death and become immortal. The extinction of the human race would then be responsible for even more loss of happiness.

The extinction of humankind is thus such a serious threat that it trumps all other concerns – even if the possibility that it will occur is infinitesimally small. It trumps the global financial crisis. It trumps climate change. It trumps the breakdown of our political or economic systems. It trumps even the worst dangers that Trump may bring about. Since it is such a large risk, we are obliged to elevate the risk of super-intelligence above all other concerns – just as in Pascal's wager, where eternal happiness and its loss elevates the risk of not believing in God above all other actions. In both cases we must ignore all other risks.

DISCOUNTING THE FUTURE

In fact, modern decision theory offers a way to counter Pascal's wager. The fix is to value the present but discount the future. Being rewarded today is more valuable than receiving the same reward tomorrow. We live in the present and not in the future. This requires us to take a rather hard-headed and utilitarian view of rewards. But it is perhaps a viewpoint that aligns with our biology. Immediate satisfaction trumps longer term benefits.

One simple way to discount the future is by means of a discount factor.[20] Suppose we discount future happiness by 2 per cent per year, the current rate of inflation in many developed economies. That is, being happy in one year's time is only 98 per cent as valuable to you as being happy today. We shall also take a simple utilitarian perspective, in which we sum up the happiness of the population. Giving two people the same happiness is twice as valuable as giving one person that happiness.

For the sake of the argument, let's suppose that the world population continues to grow at the current rate. Next year, the world population will be about 1.1 per cent larger than it is today. As the discount factor is larger than the rate of growth of the world population, the (even infinite) future population no longer dominates where the mass of happiness lies.

In sixty-three years, the world's current population will have doubled. But the discount factor on happiness now against happiness tomorrow means that the happiness of a person in sixty-three years' time is worth about a quarter of their happiness today. The discounted happiness of this doubled population is thus worth only about half of the total happiness of the world population today. So it's more important to make the world happy today than in sixty-three years' time.

In 126 years, the world's current population will have quadrupled. Because of the discount factor, though, the happiness of a person in 126 years is worth about one-sixteenth of a person's happiness today. So the discounted happiness of this quadrupled population is worth about a quarter of the total happiness of the world population in the present moment. Again, we see that it's more important to make the world happy today than in 126 years' time.

Even a small discount factor focuses our attention on the present. And there are many very immediate risks that we should worry about today. These risks will hurt us long before superintelligence. Indeed, this book is a warning about the multiple real dangers posed by AI, many of which are already starting to damage society. Most of them require only the stupid AI we have today, and not the smart AI we will likely have in fifty or 100 years' time.

NEVER SAY NEVER

Of course, we cannot confidently say that super-intelligence will never be an existential threat to humanity. History certainly offers lots of lessons about never saying never.

My colleague Stuart Russell likes to note that one of the most respected physicists of his day, Ernest Rutherford, declared that extracting energy from the atom was 'moonshine' and would never be possible. He was quoted saying this in an article published in *The Times* on 12 September 1933. The next day, Leo Szilard conceived the idea for the nuclear chain reaction, which gave us both the nuclear bomb and nuclear power.[21] We went from 'never' to 'frighteningly real' in under twenty-four hours.

We should be cautious about saying 'never'. Arthur C. Clarke proposed three laws warning of the danger of listening to experts predicting something would never happen. They are worth bearing in mind when considering the future:

- FIRST LAW: When a distinguished but elderly scientist states that something is possible, he is almost certainly right. When he states that something is impossible, he is very probably wrong.

- SECOND LAW: The only way of discovering the limits of the possible is to venture a little way past them into the impossible.

- **THIRD LAW**: Any sufficiently advanced technology is indistinguishable from magic.

So let me merely state that the technological singularity is not impossible, and you can decide what to make of that prediction!

ESCAPING BIOLOGY

Actually, the technological singularity is a bit of a distraction from the core ideas of super-intelligence. We could get to super-intelligence without passing through any sort of singularity. Machines could, for example, become super-intelligent simply by avoiding our biological limitations. Machines have many advantages over humans, some of which I listed in the last chapter.

Evolution has had to accommodate various biological constraints. For instance, our brains are restricted in size to around 100 billion neurons. And while the brain consumes more energy than any other organ in our body, it is limited to around 20 watts of power. Computers have no such limits. Want more memory? Simply add some more memory chips. Even more? Store the data on the cloud. Want more power? Simply draw more amps from the power socket in the wall. And unlike humans, computers can work 24/7. No need for rest or sleep.

Humans are limited in what they can sense. We can't hear as well as dogs or see as well as eagles. Computers can be superhuman by overcoming these limitations. They can call upon new sensors.

Infrared vision like that found in mosquitos. Ultrasonic sensing like that used by bats. Sensors not found in nature, such as GPS, radar and lidar. Machines can easily acquire superpowers.

This is why autonomous cars will be much better drivers than humans by 2062. It won't simply be because they are technically more skilled, though that is certainly going to be the case. They will, in addition, be able to calculate stopping distances far more accurately than we can. They will never be in the wrong gear. They will never break the road rules. Their radar and lidar will sense the road much better than human eyes, especially in bad weather. Their GPS will never be lost. In thirty years' time, machines will be so much better drivers than us that we may only permit human drivers on racetracks and other very controlled environments.

Autonomous cars in 2062 will also be better drivers because of their superhuman concentration. They will never tire, and never get distracted. They will be 100 per cent focused on driving, 100 per cent of the time. I don't want a super-intelligence driving my car that is also worrying about how to fix climate change and bring peace to the Middle East. I want a computer whose only goal is driving.

BRAIN INTERFACES

Elon Musk has suggested that, to keep up with machines, our only hope is to create a fast and direct interface to our brains. He's founded a start-up to develop a 'neural lace' that will connect our brains directly to computers. I find Musk's argument that this will allow us to keep up with machines unconvincing, for a number of reasons.

First, you already have a very fast interface into your brain: your eyes. It's estimated that the human eyes have a data rate of about 10 million bytes per second. That's around the speed of the ethernet port connecting your computer to the internet.

Second, the data rate into the brain doesn't seem to be a limiting factor in human cognition. You will likely learn much more from reading a textbook for two hours than watching a movie for the same length of time. But reading for two hours might only provide input of around 10 megabytes, compared to 2 gigabytes for the movie. The data rate into the brain doesn't seem to be holding us back. Learning involves abstraction, and the textbook is a better and more compact abstraction.

Third, a large portion of your brain is already dedicated to processing input data. It's estimated that around one-third of the brain is devoted to processing vision. The idea that we have large unused parts of our brain that might process additional input from some neural lace is myth.

Fourth, interfacing your brain to a machine is only likely to slow down the machine. We have almost no examples of human and machine being better together than human or machine alone. For a short while, human and computer were better at playing chess than human or computer alone. But now chess computers are so much better than us, we just get in the way. A faster interface will only expose our limitations. And if you're worried about the machines taking over, this might not be a good idea!

It is true we don't have a fast interface to output information from the brain. We only have a fast interface to input information. Speaking or typing only lets us output kilobytes of information per minute. But there doesn't seem to be a lot of evidence that this slow output speed is holding our brains back. I don't know about you, but I can already type and speak about as fast as I can think.

KEEPING AHEAD OF THE MACHINES

If a faster interface isn't the way for humans to stay ahead of the machines, what is? We need to play to our strengths – to our creativity, our adaptability, our emotional and social intelligence. But above all, we need to play to all those things that make humans special. Our art. Our love. Our laughter. Our sense of justice and fair play. Our courage and resilience. Our optimism. Our grit. Our human spirit. Our community.

It doesn't matter how smart the machines become, they will always be machines. The human experience will remain uniquely human. *Homo digitalis* will hopefully exploit this, outsourcing those tasks that machines do best to machines, and focusing on the human experience.

0003

THE END OF CONSCIOUSNESS

A very special part of us is our consciousness. From the moment we wake in the morning to the time we fall asleep at night, our consciousness is central to our experience of life. It goes to the heart of who we are. We are not just intelligent, we are aware that we are intelligent. We reflect on who we are. We worry. We remember the past. We plan the future.

At times, this constant awareness becomes so oppressive that we seek out experiences to distract our conscious mind. To live simply in the moment. We meditate. Play music. Run marathons. Drink alcohol. Base-jump off cliffs.

What is consciousness? How is it connected to intelligence? Will machines ever be conscious? By 2062, might AI even let us upload our conscious minds to the cloud? Will *Homo digitalis* have a consciousness that is part biological and part digital?

THE HARD PROBLEM

The Australian philosopher David Chalmers has called consciousness the 'hard problem'. Some have even argued that the problem is too hard for our limited minds, or that it lies outside the domain of scientific inquiry altogether. Chalmers does believe consciousness will eventually be understood scientifically, but in 1995 he argued that we are currently missing something important: 'To account for conscious experience, we need an extra ingredient in the explanation. This makes for a challenge to those who are serious about the hard problem of consciousness: What is your extra ingredient, and why should that account for conscious experience?'[1]

Some years later, he observed that:

Consciousness poses the most baffling problem in the science of the mind. There is nothing that we know more intimately than conscious experience, but there is nothing that is harder to explain. All sorts of mental phenomena have yielded to scientific investigation in recent years, but consciousness has stubbornly resisted. Many have tried to explain it, but the explanations always seem to fall short of the target.[2]

We have no instruments for measuring consciousness. As far as we can tell, there is no single part of the brain responsible for consciousness. Each of us is aware of being conscious – and, given our biological kinship, most of us are prepared to accept that other people are conscious too.

We even attribute limited levels of consciousness to certain animals. Dogs have a level of consciousness, as do cats. But not many of us think that ants have anything much in the way of consciousness. If you look at the machines we build today, then you can be pretty sure that they have absolutely no consciousness.

AlphaGo won't wake up one morning and think, 'You know what? You humans are really no good at Go. I'm going to make myself some money playing online poker instead.' In fact, AlphaGo doesn't even know it is playing Go. It will only ever do one thing: maximise its estimate of the probability that it will win the current game. And it certainly won't wake up and think, 'Actually, I'm tired of playing games. I'm going to take over the planet.' AlphaGo has no other goals than maximising the probability of winning. It has no desires. It is and only ever will be a Go-playing program. It won't be sad when it loses, or happy when it wins.

But we can't be sure that this situation won't change. Perhaps in the future we will build machines that will be conscious. To behave ethically, it may be very important that computers can reflect on their decisions. To act in a changing and uncertain world, it may be necessary to build machines with very open goals,

77

and an ability to reflect on how to achieve and even adapt those goals. These may be steps on the road to a conscious machine.

Consciousness is such an important part of our existence that we must wonder if it has given us a strong evolutionary advantage. Our complex societies work in part because we are conscious of how others might be thinking. And if consciousness has been such a strong evolutionary advantage in humans, it might be useful to give machines that advantage.

CONSCIOUS MACHINES

Consciousness in machines might come about in one of three ways: it might be programmed, it might emerge out of complexity, or it might be learned.

The first route seems difficult. How do we program something that we understand so poorly? It might be enough to wrap an executive layer on top of the machine that monitors its actions and its reasoning. Or we might have to wait until we understand consciousness better before we can begin to program it.

Alternatively, consciousness might not need to be explicitly programmed. It might simply be an emergent phenomenon. We have plenty of examples of emergent phenomena in complex systems. Life, for example, emerged out of our complex universe. Consciousness might similarly emerge out of a sufficiently complex machine. It is certainly the case in nature that consciousness is correlated with larger and more complex brains. We know so little about consciousness that we cannot discount the possibility that it might emerge out of a sufficiently complex AI system.

The third option – that machines learn to be conscious – is also not unreasonable. Much of *our* consciousness appears to be learned. When we are born, we have limited consciousness. We appear to take delight in discovering our toes. It takes a number of months, if not a year or more, before we realise that our image in a mirror is, in fact, us. If we learn our sense of self, could not a machine do the same?

Consciousness might, however, be something you cannot simulate in a machine. It might be a property of the right sort of matter. An analogy is weather. You can simulate a storm in a computer, but it will never be wet inside the computer. In a similar way, consciousness might only come about with the right arrangement of matter. And silicon might not be the right sort of matter to have consciousness.

ZOMBIE INTELLIGENCE

When I talk to people about artificial intelligence, they often focus on the second word, 'intelligence'. After all, intelligence is what makes us special, and intelligence is what AI is trying to build. But I also remind people to think about the word 'artificial'. In 2062 we might end up having built a very different – a very *artificial* – kind of intelligence distinct from the natural intelligence that we have. It might not, for instance, be a conscious intelligence.

Flight is a good analogy. As humans, we have been very successful at building artificial flight. We have built aeroplanes that can fly faster than the speed of sound, cross oceans in hours and carry tonnes of cargo. If we had tried to recreate natural flight, I imagine we'd still be at the end of the runway flapping our wings. We came at the problem of flight from a completely different angle to nature – with a fixed wing and a powerful engine. Both natural and artificial flight depend on the same theory of aerodynamics, but they are different solutions to the challenge of flying. And nature neither necessarily finds the easiest or the best solution.[3]

Similarly, compared to natural intelligence, artificial intelligence might be a very different solution to the problem. One way in which it might be different is that it might be an unconscious form of intelligence. David Chalmers has called this 'zombie intelligence'. We might build AIs that are intelligent, even super-intelligent, but lacking in any form of consciousness. They would definitely appear to us as *artificial* intelligence. Zombie intelligence would demonstrate that intelligence and consciousness were somewhat separate phenomena. We would have intelligence without consciousness. But unless you could develop consciousness without intelligence, which seems even more unlikely, zombie intelligence would not show that the two phenomena were completely separable. One implies the other, but not vice versa.

Zombie intelligence would be a lucky ethical break for humankind. If AI was only a zombie intelligence, then we might not have to worry about how we treat machines. We could have machines do the most tedious and repetitive tasks. We could switch them off without worrying that they would suffer. On the other hand, if AI is not a type of zombie intelligence, we may have to make some challenging ethical decisions. If machines become conscious, do they have rights? Campaigns are already underway to grant legal personhood to great apes, such as chimpanzees and gorillas. Would intelligent machines gain similar rights if they were conscious? Should we still be able to switch them off?

THE AMAZING OCTOPUS

Humans are not the only conscious life on the planet. Nature has found at least two different routes to intelligence and consciousness. Cephalopods – especially the Coleoidea subclass, which consists of invertebrates such as the octopus – have a fundamentally different type of nervous system to vertebrates. Cephalopods are thought to be the most intelligent of all invertebrates.

This might not sound impressive, as a number of invertebrates, such as clams, have no brain at all. But cephalopod intelligence is astounding. They use tools. They cooperate and communicate when hunting together. They can open screw-capped jars. Cephalopods even appear to be able to recognise and remember people. It was claimed that Otto, a famous octopus at the Sea Star Aquarium in Coburg, Germany, could turn an annoying 2000-watt spotlight off at night by squirting water at it. There are many other anecdotal examples of their problem-solving ability, including their propensity to escape from holding tanks.

Due to their intelligence, cephalopods have been given protection from scientific testing in several countries. In the United Kingdom, the common octopus was the only invertebrate protected by the *Animals (Scientific Procedures) Act 1986*. And in Europe, cephalopods are the only invertebrates protected by the 2010 European directive concerning the protection of animals in scientific experiments.

Cephalopods diverged from humans around 600 million years ago, long before the dinosaurs roamed the planet. At that time, the most complex animals only had a few neurons each. Cephalopods developed their intelligence in an entirely separate way to us. Three-fifths of an octopus's neurons are in its eight legs. Each leg can sense and think independently of the rest. In a way, it's as if each leg has its own brain. It's hard to imagine what it must be like to be an octopus when your legs are all doing their own thing – perhaps it would be a little like being drunk.

This strange exotic form of intelligence reminds us that AI may one day have a very different intelligence to ours. Even if we build an AI that is conscious, it may still be a very *artificial* intelligence compared to ours. And this, again, may be a lucky ethical break.

Cows, pigs and many of the other animals we have domesticated have a certain amount of intelligence and consciousness. But, in part because they are sufficiently 'different' to us, we seem prepared to overlook the challenging ways that we treat them. In a similar way, we may be willing to treat an *artificial* intelligence in ways that would be unacceptable if it were human.

PAINFUL PROBLEMS

Machines today don't suffer pain. This is perhaps unsurprising, as machines are not conscious and pain seems intimately connected to consciousness. Human rights can be seen as a moral response to preventing pain and suffering. So without pain, perhaps machines have no rights?

From a technological perspective, it may be useful for machines in 2062 to experience pain. Whether this should be real pain, like ours, or artificial pain is open to debate. Pain has a long evolutionary history, and appears to have served both humans and other animals well. Pain might help robots learn quickly from their mistakes. We move our hand away from the fire quickly not because we recognise the damage done by the fire, but because of the intensity of the pain. Robots might benefit from similar feedback mechanisms.

But giving machines pain could also backfire. They might then become able to suffer, and so deserve rights to prevent their suffering. This would greatly limit their usefulness as we might not be able to force them to do our dirtiest and most dangerous work. And if we give robots pain, perhaps we should also give them fear, which often precedes pain and also prevents injury. And why stop there? Might it not be useful to give robots other human emotions, such as desire, happiness, interest, surprise, wonder or even sorrow?

Humans have rich emotional lives. Indeed, our emotions and our intelligence seem intimately connected. Much of our behaviour is driven by our emotions. Emotions would appear to offer a significant evolutionary advantage: surprise helps us identify the new and potentially dangerous; curiosity drives us to discover and command the world. Would we not want machines to have these advantages?

Machines today have no emotions. They are, however, starting to be given a rudimentary understanding of human emotions. They can, for example, decide whether the text of an email is angry. This will help them interact with us in the long-running conversation we will have with machines.

The movie *Her* got it spot-on. Artificial intelligence is the operating system of 2062. We will increasingly interact with all the connected devices in our lives by speaking to them. There won't be any keyboards, just speech for input and output. And this conversation will follow you from room to room, to your car, to your office and back to your home.

To make these conversations more engaging, technologists will be tempted to give machines emotional lives of their own. Again, whether these are real or fake emotions is up for debate. But it seems highly likely that the intelligent machines that will interact with us in 2062 will be emotional.

Marvin, the paranoid android in Douglas Adams' *The Hitchhiker's Guide to the Galaxy*, expressed this well: 'And then of course

I've got this terrible pain in all the diodes down my left-hand side ...' As well as having painful diodes, he was also a famously depressed robot:

ARTHUR DENT: [Earth] was a beautiful place.

MARVIN: Did it have oceans?

ARTHUR DENT: Oh yes; great wide rolling blue oceans.

MARVIN: Can't bear oceans.

These rather human traits endeared Marvin to thousands of fans of *The Hitchhiker's Guide*. By 2062 we can expect to be having our emotions moved by many other machines.

THE PROBLEM OF FREE WILL

Even if consciousness proves not to be a problem for AI, we have to consider another thorny and related philosophical problem. The problem of free will. Artificial intelligence throws a harsh light on this old challenge, as computers are deterministic machines. They follow precise instructions. Digital devices such as computers are arguably our most deterministic inventions.

In an analog device, such as a thermostat, there are tolerances and uncertainties that mean it may behave in unexpected ways. Even simple systems can have chaotic feedback loops that may make predicting behaviours impossible. In a digital device, there are no such ambiguities. States are either 0 or 1. There is no uncertainty or chance. Computers are a physical interpretation of mathematical logic, so they're as exact and unambiguous as logic. Add 1 and 1 together, and you'll always get 2. Ask for the square root of 9, and you'll always get 3.

How, then, can an AI, a program running on a deterministic computer, have any sort of free will? Free will is one of those topics that many scientists are careful to avoid. As scientists, most of us go to bed at night knowing that we cannot really explain it. We develop mathematical equations that govern precisely when a neuron fires. We posit chemical pathways that have precise outcomes. We discuss ion transfers that are driven by exact differential equations. Where in these models of the brain is there room for free will?

Free will is not a problem restricted to AI. It is something that science struggles to explain in our own biological brains. Our scientific models of the brain leave gaps where free will might be hiding. One place is in quantum strangeness.

Sir Roger Penrose, one of the most vocal critics against the possibility of artificial intelligence, has argued that the brain is not algorithmic, and cannot be modelled by a conventional digital computer. He conjectures that quantum effects play an essential role in the human brain.[4] The scientific jury is still out on whether quantum effects do play this essential role. But even if they do, there's nothing stopping a digital computer from simulating quantum effects, leading us to wonder if Penrose has perhaps actually found a place for a ghost to hide.

Another place that free will might be hiding is in the complexity of the world in which we interact. Free will might just be something that emerges from the interaction between people and the environment. As Daniel Dennett has argued, free will might simply be an illusion that emerges from this complexity.

We often fail to remember that a complex world is shaping our decision-making. What appears to us as free will is nothing more than the result of a large, very complex system in which we are just small bit players. Whether it turns out that free will is real or an illusion, AI may help us get to the bottom of this mystery.

ETHICAL ROBOTS

If intelligent machines do get to have free will, then we will have to be be concerned about their values. Will they use this free will to do evil? Even without free will, we will want intelligent machines to behave ethically.

The problem here isn't just *smart* machines. We'd also want a very stupid AI to behave ethically. Indeed, we have this problem today with autonomous cars. These are not very intelligent, yet. But we are already letting them make life or death decisions.

When it comes to behaving ethically a conscious machine will have some advantage over an unconscious one. It can reflect on its actions, both past, present and future. It can reflect on how others will be impacted by these actions. It's hard to imagine building a robot that behaves ethically without an executive layer that acts, in some way, like conscious human selves.

87

What should go in this executive layer that governs how a robot acts? Should we perhaps program something like Asimov's three laws of robotics? Isaac Asimov proposed his famous laws back in 1942.

- **FIRST LAW**: A robot may not injure a human being or, through inaction, allow a human being to come to harm.

- **SECOND LAW**: A robot must obey the orders given it by human beings except where such orders would conflict with the First Law.

- **THIRD LAW**: A robot must protect its own existence as long as such protection does not conflict with the First or Second Laws.

Asimov claimed these laws came from the *Handbook of Robotics*, fifty-sixth edition, published in 2058. I'm sure that by 2058 Asimov will be right and there'll be well-defined ethical guidelines for building robots. But if Asimov's stories do anything, they demonstrate the limitations of his three laws. What happens if taking action will harm one person but doing nothing will harm another? What happens if two humans issue conflicting orders?

The classic trolley problem is an example of the sort of moral dilemma that challenges Asimov's laws. Suppose you are sitting in your Tesla, which is driving along the road autonomously. Suddenly two young children run onto the road, chasing a ball. Does the Tesla drive into the two children or swerve into a parked car? The computer has milliseconds to decide which action to take, all of which may result in injury or even death. There isn't time to give control back to you. Doing nothing will likely kill the children. But taking evasive action by swerving into the parked car will likely kill you. Asimov's laws don't help the Tesla decide what to do.

The limitations of Asimov's laws are highlighted by his later introduction of a fourth law.

- **ZEROTH LAW**: A robot may not harm humanity, or, by inaction, allow humanity to come to harm.

This law is numbered zero, as it takes precedence over the previous three laws. The law captures the fact that there are situations in which a robot harming a human may be the best action for a robot. But it still leaves uncertain what precisely to do in our Tesla-trolley problem.

Asimov's zeroth law actually creates a fresh set of problems. How can a robot decide what will harm humanity? What does it even mean to harm humanity? How, for instance, do we trade off the welfare of humans alive from those yet to be born?

I suspect we may fail to program by hand the ethics of our intelligent machines. We may decide instead to let the machines learn to behave ethically. This is not without its challenges. We humans often act in ways that don't meet the ethical standards we have set for ourselves. Machines will therefore have difficulty learning ethics by observing human behaviour.

In fact, we probably should hold machines to higher ethical standards than humans. They have none of our human weaknesses. An autonomous car can be programmed never to speed. An autonomous and armed drone can be programmed always to follow international humanitarian law. And a robot lawyer can be programmed never to hide discovered evidence. It's an interesting and open question: how would such super-ethics be learned?

THE END OF DEATH

Our consciousness is intimately connected with our being alive. And as far as current science can tell us, consciousness appears to end with death. This brings us, then, to the subject of death. And to get to death, we will go via transhumanism.

Artificial intelligence today has gone pretty mainstream. Twenty years ago, when I told people I was working on artificial intelligence they would laugh and joke about how stupid computers were. But now, as AI is starting to infiltrate into, and even improve, parts of our lives, people often say, 'You work in AI – cool!' Artificial general intelligence, on the other hand, still remains a fringe pursuit. And if you start exploring that fringe, one place you may end up at is transhumanism. Here you find people who see AI as a way to cheat death itself.

Interestingly, many of the more vocal in warning about the existential risk posed by AI, people such as Nick Bostrom, are transhumanists. Of course, this should not be too surprising. If you are planning on living forever, then you have a lot to lose personally if AI were to extinguish the human race. It is therefore amusingly ironic to see transhumanists who are keen to see AI as soon as possible, as it will help them achieve their transhumanist dreams, but who are equally fearful of what AI may do.

How might AI be the end of death? Our biological selves are very imperfect vessels. Viruses and bacterial infections invade our defences. Our immune systems break, letting cancers take hold and kill us. Our repair mechanisms stop working, leaving us old and decrepit. After three score years and ten, most of us are en route to the mortuary. Silicon would make a far superior host for our intelligence. It's faster, more capacious and largely free from decay. And since digital information can be copied without error, we can always reboot onto a new and perfect host.

So in 2062, will we simply upload our brains into the cloud and take on a virtual existence? Given the superior characteristics of a digital substrate, will *Homo digitalis* be completely digital? Or will *Homo digitalis* remain part biological and part digital? The answers to these questions depend to some degree on the nature of consciousness. If consciousness is uniquely biological, then uploading ourselves to the cloud will leave something important behind. Our zombie self might appear to be us. It will know all that we know. It will say all the things that we would say. But it will not be *us*. On the other hand, if AI can be conscious, then perhaps our uploaded self might inherit a consciousness similar to that of our biological self. This is an altogether more troubling possibility.

Fortunately, we may be saved from the ethical dilemmas that uploading our brains would present by technological limitations. It might simply be impossible or impractical to read the contents of our biological brains accurately enough to make a digital copy. The human brain, with its billions of neurons and trillions of synapses, is the most complex system we know of in the universe by orders of magnitude. It simply might not be technically feasible to 'read' each of these. Alternatively, it might be possible but only destructively so. That is, we can read the contents of our brains but in doing so we destroy the original. In this way, we might be able to create an artificial copy but not have a working biological brain left behind. This would save us from some difficult moral and ethical questions about identity and self.

VIRTUAL LIFE

My expectation is that we'll keep our biological form but augment it with digital assistants that will constantly help out. We'll also have digital avatars, which will sound and act like us in the digital world. And by 2062 we'll be immersing ourselves in virtual and augmented worlds that will be impossible to distinguish from the real world. Even though our physical bodies will be in the real world, our brains will think they are in the digital one.

These virtual worlds will be very seductive. All of us can be rich and famous, in such worlds. We can all be beautiful and smart. We can all be successful. Nothing will be beyond us.

The real world will be decidedly less pleasant. Not surprisingly, some of us will become addicted to escaping reality in this way, spending every waking moment in virtual worlds. We can already see such trends emerging in the developed world. During the 2000s, men in the United States between the ages of twenty-one and thirty with less than a bachelor's degree experienced a 20 per cent decline in hours worked. At the same time, many of these men are spending an increasing amount of time playing video games. Indeed, many spend more time playing video games than socialising with friends, playing sports or doing other hobbies. This group makes up 40 per cent of the total gaming population between the ages of twenty-one and fifty-five, despite representing only 10 per cent of that age segment of the population. For this group, the virtual world increasingly appears to be offering a virtual escape from the real world.

A disturbing aspect of virtual worlds will be that some people will inhabit them in order to act in ways that are not acceptable in the real world. Society will have to decide if behaviours which are illegal in the real world should be made illegal or impossible in the virtual. Alternatively, society may decide that such virtual worlds provide a necessary safety valve. It will be a difficult decision to make, and I expect opinion will swing back and forth.

THE END OF BIOLOGY

Another way that we might end death is by defeating biology. AI will help us understand more about how the human body works, and about how to stop and even reverse ageing. Perhaps we will simply cure all diseases that afflict us, including the disease that ends most of our lives in the Western world: old age.

Why do we live three score years and ten, not thirty score years and ten? And if we can get to thirty score years, why stop there? For the first half of our lives, our bodies are remarkably good at repairing themselves. Perhaps we can trick the body into doing this for a longer time? Combined with new gene-editing technologies such as CRISPR[5], AI might help us down the road towards immortality.

Such a change to human existence will require profound changes to society. If this 'immortality' is limited to the rich, our society will become even more divided, between the rich immortals and the poor mortals. Rich people already live longer than poor people, but such a stark difference is likely to cause much social dissent.

On the other hand, if immortality of this kind is available to all, we will need to reimagine completely how we run society. Will we need to introduce voluntary euthanasia to make room for new generations? Will we need a zero-child policy, and perhaps a lottery to decide when you can have children to replace those who accidentally or purposefully die? How will we reinvent the cycle of childhood, work and retirement for lives that might last hundreds or even thousands of years?

Life without end will also require us to reconsider the meaning of our existence. The human experience is defined by its brevity. Life is short, and this is part of its beauty. We must live life to the full, for none of us knows when it will end. And we all share the same ultimate fate. If *Homo digitalis* transcends this, we may need entirely new beliefs to give life meaning.

0004

THE END OF WORK

L et us not forget that 'work' is the only truly obscene four-letter word. One of the most visible impacts of artificial intelligence in 2062 will be that humans will be doing much less work. The future may simply give us what some rich people have today: lives of leisure.

It might be called the Second Renaissance, for it will be the machines that are sweating, while we focus our time on more important things than simply feeding and housing ourselves. We will be making and enjoying great art. We will be nurturing and growing our communities, and engaging in healthy and strong political debate. And we will be protecting and enjoying our beautiful planet. Some of us might even use all this free time to become amateur scientists. We will be discovering more of the wonders of the universe – helped, no doubt, by machine assistants. Like the last Renaissance, it will be a time where knowledge of our place in the universe expands rapidly.

All in all, life will be good. The price of the basic goods we need will have fallen dramatically, as they'll be produced by more efficient machines. Poverty will be a distant memory – as it is for those of us in the developed world who have distant memories of the poorhouse of the Victorian era. And those of us who still choose to work will have four- or five-day weekends. All of us will share the wealth created by the machines that never sleep.

Looking back from 2062, the year 2000 will look very old-fashioned. It's worth remembering just how dramatically even developed countries such as Australia, the United States and the United Kingdom changed between 1900 and 1962. It's quite possible our lives will change equivalently between 2000 and 2062.

In 1900 the streets were full of horses and carts. Many of us worked in dreadful conditions, doing repetitive and tedious work. The life expectancy for someone born in that year was just forty-one years. If we wind forward sixty-two years, we were on course to go to the Moon, the streets were full of cars and trucks, and working conditions had improved substantially. The jet age had begun, and the world was shrinking fast. It was an optimistic time, after the upset of two world wars and the Great Depression. Science was bringing noticeable benefits to our lives, and there was a feeling that society was set to improve greatly. The period known as the 'swinging sixties' was around the corner.

Life expectancy had nearly doubled, to seventy-one years.

The year 2062 might be a similarly optimistic time. We may have suffered nearly fifty years of pain as we adjust to the new technologies, but the machines will now be taking much of the strain and life will have improved immensely. Poverty will have been eliminated. Life expectancy will be 100 years or more. The year 2000 will truly seem like another age.

HALF OF ALL JOBS

One of the concerns that economists have today is that many jobs are simply going to disappear by 2062. A lot of our work will be automated out of existence. Will this be the end of work? If the machines can outperform us, both mentally and physically, what will be left for humans to do?

This is not a small fear. In October 2017 Google announced that it would spend $1 billion over the next five years through the 'Grow with Google' program to retrain workers in America with new skills, to help local and small businesses grow, and to support non-profits around the world working in these areas. Google employees also will volunteer 1 million hours at those non-profits.

Many fears about job displacement can be traced to a 2013 study of the impact of automation, by Carl B. Frey and Michael A. Osborne of the University of Oxford. The study made a much-quoted prediction that 47 per cent of jobs in the United States were under threat from automation over the next two decades.

Other more recent and detailed studies have made similarly dramatic predictions.

It has to be said that such predictions have been made by economists at regular intervals throughout most of the last century. Back in 1930, for example, John Maynard Keynes warned of 'a new disease of which some readers may not have heard the name, but of which they will hear a great deal in the years to come: namely, technological unemployment.' Economists tend to be wrong quite often, so perhaps it should not be surprising that these earlier predictions did not eventuate. Despite Keynes' warning, unemployment today is at historically low levels in most countries. And this is notwithstanding the world's population being at historically high levels. Work hasn't ended – indeed, there appears to be much more work going on. And many of us seem to be spending more and more time doing it.

Two things stand out from the Frey and Osborne report. First, the report itself was largely automated. The authors used machine learning to predict precisely which of over 700 different jobs could be automated. It is of course ironic that a report about the automation of work was itself largely automated; it seems we had to wait until the machines started telling us that we would be automated before we were prepared to listen seriously.

The second thing that stands out from the Frey and Osborne report is that the number of jobs predicted to be at risk of automation is spectacularly large. Nearly half of all jobs are predicted to be at risk. This created a meme that has been repeated frequently.

Andy Haldane, the chief economist of the Bank of England, predicted in November 2015 that around half of all jobs in the United Kingdom were at risk of automation. And in October 2016 Jim Yong Kim, president of the World Bank, predicted that 69 per cent of jobs in India and 77 per cent of jobs in China are at risk. With large numbers like this, it's no surprise that many of us have started to worry.

Before we go on, let's put to rest once and for all the percentage of jobs at risk. Anyone who claims to be able to predict the number of jobs at risk in the next two decades, especially to the precision of 47 per cent, 69 per cent or 77 per cent, is fooling themselves, and trying to fool you too. We have no real idea about the number of jobs at risk; there are just too many uncertainties.

TRAINING DATA

One reason that predictions such as those of Frey and Osborne and the World Bank and others are likely wrong is because of errors in the input – the training data. There's a well-known saying in computing: garbage in, garbage out.

In this case, the predictions of the classifier in the Frey and Osborne study depend critically on the training data. The researchers classified by hand whether seventy of the 702 different jobs studied were at risk of automation over the next two decades. Their classification was binary: a job was either at risk of automation or not at risk of automation. Yet, some of the jobs classified likely fell in between. For instance, one job which they classified as being at risk of automation was *accountant and auditor*. They are certainly parts of being an accountant and auditor that will be automated during the next few decades, but I doubt that the job of being an accountant or auditor will disappear.

In any case, Frey and Osborne classified thirty-seven of their seventy jobs as being at risk of automation. That is, over half of their training data, provided as input to the classifier, were jobs said to be at risk of automation. Not surprisingly, then, the output of the classifier was the prediction that around half the full set of 702 jobs were at risk of automation. If their training set had been more cautious – say, labelling only one in four jobs as being at risk of automation – then it's likely their overall prediction about the full set of jobs would have been equally cautious.

In January 2017, I decided to explore this idea with a survey of my own, which I conducted when also asking AI experts to predict how long it would take before machines were as smart as humans. I asked 300 experts in AI and robotics to classify which of the jobs in Frey and Osborne's training set were at risk of automation over the next two decades. I also asked the same question of nearly 500 non-experts, members of the public who read an article I wrote about advances in poker bots. The non-experts agreed almost exactly with Frey and Osborne's predictions. But the experts in AI and robotics were significantly more cautious.[1] They predicted that around 20 per cent fewer jobs were at risk of automation than Frey and Osborne did. Of course, even this would still translate into a significant number of jobs, but it's not quite as dramatic as the Oxford study suggested.

REPAIRING BICYCLES

Even supposing we could correct Frey and Osborne's predictions with better training data, we would still not be done. For instance, their machine-learning classifier gives a 94 per cent probability that *bicycle repair person* will be automated in the next two decades. But I can assure you that there is a close to zero chance that we will have automated even small parts of this job by then.

This error throws light on some of the limitations of their study. First, bicycles are difficult, fiddly objects to repair, and have lots of non-standard parts. Second, it will not be economically viable to replace a bicycle repair person with a robot. It's not a well-paid job and it would require a very expensive robot. And third, being a bicycle repair person is a social job. It's about talking to the customer, selling them the latest kit, offering tips on good places to ride. It's not just about repairing bicycles.

The classifier used by Frey and Osborne didn't take account of whether it would be economically feasible to automate a job. It only took account of whether it was technically possible. Similarly, their classifier didn't look at whether we might simply *prefer* a human to do the job. And there are a host of other features not in their data that will decide which jobs get automated and which don't.

FLYING PLANES

Another prediction in Frey and Osborne's study is that there is a 55 per cent probability that a *commercial pilot* will be automated in the next two decades. This is an interesting prediction, as, from a technical perspective, we can already automate much of this job today. Indeed, most of the time a computer is already flying your plane. (When the landing isn't that smooth, you know the human pilot was in control.) What's more, airspace is a very controlled environment, and this makes it easier to automate planes than, say, cars.

It's not clear what this 55 per cent probability means. It's certainly unlikely that 55 per cent of all commercial pilots will have been replaced by computers in twenty years' time. Indeed, Boeing predicts that over 600,000 new pilots will be needed during that time. It might be in their interests to say so, but nonetheless, this hardly sounds like an occupation at risk. With the emerging middle class in China and India developing a taste for travel, demand for pilots is increasing. And automation seems to be having little impact on that demand.

I expect it will take more than two decades for commercial pilots to be replaced by computers. As travellers, we like the idea of having a person up front, someone whose life is also on the line if things go wrong. It will likely take more than two decades before it has become socially acceptable to leave the pilot behind. Even if most accidents are caused today by pilot error.

A couple of decades ago, when I boarded a plane, I wanted that person up front to be a silver-haired, experienced-looking pilot. There is a saying that there are old pilots, and bold pilots, but no old bold pilots. But today I look for a young nerd who knows how to drive all the screens. So the job will change. It will be more about using computers than old-fashioned flying. But the demand for human pilots seems unlikely to drop.

ROBOT MODELS

Another prediction in Frey and Osborne's study is that there's a 98 per cent probability that fashion models will be automated in the next two decades. Really? Are we really going to replace human models, with their pouts, their hip-swaying and swagger, for robots on the catwalks of the world?

Again, this sounds doubtful. We don't want to know what clothes look like on a robot, but on a person. We don't aspire to be a robot wearing an expensive watch, but to be that wealthy-looking male model. And let me not forget one technical objection: robots aren't going to be walking in high heels anytime soon.

There is one area in which human models will be replaced, and that is in the virtual world. We will be able to generate models digitally. These digital models will be indistinguishable from their human counterparts. And they'll get out of bed for much less than $10,000 per day.

The music business is suggestive of where modelling might go. Digital music didn't result in fewer human musicians. Indeed, the demand for musicians is predicted by the US Department of Labor not to decrease but to increase modestly in the next decade. The music business shifted to the analog world. Many musicians make more money now from performance than from recording. We value experiences – hearing our musical idols in person. In a similar way, we can expect modelling as an occupation will remain but become more focused on performance. And even in fashion photography, there will be a shift away from the artificial to the real. The US Department of Labor predicts that the number of people employed as models will neither decrease nor increase significantly over the next decade.

THE REAL NUMBER OF JOBS AT RISK

Frey and Osborne's classifier didn't take into account many technical, economic and social variables. Not surprisingly, their classifier predicted that low-paid jobs are at risk of automation when it's not economically viable to automate them. Even supposing we did extend their model to take account of these and many other important factors, their prediction that 47 per cent of jobs are at risk of automation does not translate into 47 per cent unemployment. There will be many new jobs created by technology, and there are other factors that need to be take into account, such as changing demographics.

The history of technology has been that more jobs are created than destroyed by new technologies. Before the Industrial

Revolution, most people worked in agriculture or as craftspeople. Many of these jobs became mechanised. But many more new jobs were created in offices and factories. Similarly, we can expect new jobs to be created as AI automates old ones.

The message is that any prediction about the number of jobs at risk of automation is inherently uncertain, as is the impact on employment levels. It is very unlikely that 47 per cent of all jobs will be automated away. The truth is that no one can say what the net effect on employment will be.

WHAT WE KNOW

There is evidence that *some* jobs are starting to be automated – and that some of these jobs are not being replaced by jobs elsewhere. An MIT study from 2017 analysed the impact of automation in the United States between 1993 and 2007. It found that industrial robots reduced jobs overall.

On average, every new robot replaced around 5.6 workers. And offsetting gains were not observed in other occupations. In fact, the study estimated that every additional robot per 1000 workers reduced the total population in employment in the United States by 0.34 percentage points.

Automation also put pressure on the jobs that remained. Every additional robot per 1000 workers reduced wages by 0.5 percentage points. During the fourteen-year period of the study, the number of industrial robots in the United States quadrupled, eliminating what they estimated was around half a million jobs.

The oil industry provides an informative case study of the scale of the challenge. The price of oil collapsed from $115 per barrel in August 2014 to below $30 at the start of 2016. This drove the industry to decrease headcount and introduce more automation. Nearly half a million jobs disappeared from the oil industry worldwide. But now, as the price of oil is rebounding, and the industry is again growing, fewer than half of those jobs have returned. Automation has reduced the twenty people typically employed at a well to just five.

OPEN VERSUS CLOSED JOBS

One reason automation won't eliminate certain jobs is that, in some cases, it will simply let us do more of that particular job. It's useful in this respect to distinguish between 'open' and 'closed' jobs. Automation will tend to augment open jobs but replace closed jobs.

Closed jobs are those where there is a fixed amount of work. For example, *window cleaner* is a closed job. There are only a fixed number of windows to be cleaned on the planet. At the CeBIT computer expo in 2017, I saw a number of prototype window-cleaning robots. Once robots can clean windows, which is not far away, the job of human window cleaner will disappear. At least, the job will disappear from developed countries, where human window cleaners are expensive and prone to falling off ladders.

Similarly, *bicycle repair person* is a closed job. I've already raised doubts about the likelihood that this job will be automated, but even if it is, there aren't suddenly going to be a lot more bicycles to repair.

Open jobs, by comparison, expand as you automate them. For instance, *chemist* is an open job. If you're a chemist, having tools that automate your job merely helps you do more chemistry. You can push back the frontiers of our understanding of chemistry that much faster. You are unlikely to run out of new chemistry to understand.

Of course, most jobs are neither completely open nor completely closed. Take the legal profession. As computers take over more and more routine legal work, the cost of accessing the law will fall. This will expand the market for lawyers, generating more demand and giving all of us better access to legal advice. Most likely it will create more work for experienced lawyers. But it's hard to imagine that there will still be lots of entry-level legal jobs. It might become harder for young graduates to compete with robo-lawyers, which have read all the legal literature, never need to sleep, never make mistakes and don't need a salary.

JOBS ONLY PARTLY AUTOMATED

One argument put forward about why the automation of 47 per cent of jobs won't translate into mass unemployment is that only *some parts* of these 47 per cent of jobs will be automated. I don't buy this argument. If you automate parts of a job, then you can usually do the same work with fewer people.

Consider again the job of a lawyer. Closer analysis of the time lawyers spend on different aspects of their work suggests that only around one-quarter of their time is spent doing tasks that might be automated in the near future.[2] Let's put aside for a second how many of the remaining tasks might be automated in the more distant future. Unless we create more legal work, then we could do the current legal work with three-quarters of the lawyers we have today. Lawyers might lift their game and use the extra time they have to do better-quality work. But some law firms will simply lower their prices by three-quarters, and cut one-quarter of their staff to compensate for their reduced income.

This argument – that only parts of jobs will be automated – has even been used to argue that one of the jobs seemingly most at risk of automation is, in fact, safe. Truck drivers need not worry, it's been argued, as there will always be edge cases that defeat the machines. The truck arrives at some engineering works where a roadworker signals to the truck by hand. The truck needs to drive around a factory that is not on any GPS maps. Autonomous trucks will simply be unable to cope with such situations.

The bad news for truck drivers is that this neglects remote driving. Companies such as Starksy Robotics are already testing autonomous trucks in which remote drivers take over when the machine cannot cope. One such remote driver will be able to take care of multiple autonomous trucks. So while we might have humans driving trucks remotely for some time to come, there will be many fewer of them than now.

WORKING LESS

Another reason that 47 per cent automation won't translate into 47 per cent unemployment is that we might just work a shorter week. That was the case during the Industrial Revolution. Before then, many of us would wake up with the sun, go out into the fields and work till the sun went down, and then go to bed. Many worked around sixty hours per week. After the Industrial Revolution, work reduced to around forty hours per week for most people. And some of us even got a few weeks of vacation each year.

The same could happen with the AI Revolution. We could shorten the working day. Or we could have a three-day or four-day weekend. But this would require some of the wealth generated by increasing productivity to be shared around, and there is little evidence that this sharing of wealth is starting to happen. Indeed, the evidence appears to suggest the opposite. Wage growth for most workers in developed economies has stopped, or is failing to keep up with the limited inflation we now experience.

There's an argument that we could afford to work less. AI will bring down the price of many basic necessities. More efficient machines will make many of life's essentials cheaper. So we might not need wage growth in order to work less. We could – in theory, at least – live on less.

VALUING ALL WORK

In addition to working less, we could also pay people more for the work that they already do. Many of us look after elderly relatives, raise children and volunteer in our communities. This is all work that is vital to society, but is often unpaid. As society grows richer, we ought to find ways to compensate people for such work. To value it more. Many of us derive status in society through the paid work we do. We see ourselves as hardworking, tax-paying, contributing members of our communities. We need to respect those who do this unpaid work, which is vital to keeping society running smoothly.

This reflects a wider problem. There are many paid and unpaid jobs which we should value more, among them teachers, nurses, policemen and policewomen, firemen and firewomen, and many others who we can't do without. The productivity bonus that AI brings could, if we choose, be invested in ways that recognise and reward such roles.

AN AGEING PLANET

We must also consider our changing demographics. In many developed countries, for instance, people are having fewer children, and people are living longer. Retirement ages are going up as a consequence, but typically not by as much as life expectancy is rising.

My colleague Rodney Brooks, one of the most famous roboticists alive, has said that he doesn't worry about technological unemployment. In fact, he believes quite the opposite. He reckons the robots will only arrive just in time to save us from this crunch. Without the robots, there will be no one left to do all the work that will support all these retired people.

Japan is one of the places at the centre of this change. The Japanese have one of the longest life expectancies on the planet, and Japanese companies are investing heavily in building care robots. Japanese society seems especially welcoming to the idea of using robots to care for the elderly and the rest of the world may eventually follow its lead. If Rodney Brooks is right, we might have no choice. But supposing we do, are these not jobs we want to reserve for humans? Do we really want to be looked after by robots in our old age?

WINNERS AND LOSERS

Technologies tend to impact different groups differently, and AI will doubtlessly follow this pattern. Some groups will be advantaged and others disadvantaged. Who, then, will be the winners and losers?

One group that looks set to lose are twenty-something males without a tertiary education. In 2015, 22 per cent of American men aged between twenty-one and thirty and without a college degree had not worked at all during the previous twelve months. This demographic used to be the backbone of the workforce.

They were the most reliable and hardworking cohort of workers in America. They would get a blue-collar job straight out of school, and work continuously until retirement. Today, more than one in five are out of work and, in many cases, not looking for it.

Without jobs, this group is less likely to marry, to leave home or to engage politically. Many are sitting at home, lost in virtual worlds. Their death rate has increased as many seek refuge in drink and drugs. If they cannot get on the employment ladder, are they going to be without a decent job forever? The future for them looks rather bleak.

SEA OF DUDES

Another group that is losing out are women. We already have a name for this problem: the 'sea of dudes'. The name was coined in 2016 by Margaret Mitchell, then an AI researcher at Microsoft Research and now at Google. It highlights the fact that only around 10 per cent of AI researchers are women. This gender imbalance is harmful to progress in developing AI. Some fundamental problems won't be addressed because basic questions are not even asked. Shouldn't a medical app take account of a women's menstrual cycle?[3] In a recruitment tool, how can we eliminate bias against people who have taken parental leave?

More generally, women will lose out as many of the new jobs created will involve technology. If the gender imbalance in technology jobs remains, then women will be at a disadvantage in winning future new jobs. On the other hand, more men may be working in jobs at risk of automation than women. It is unclear which of these two competing factors will be decisive.

Women are not the only large group that are currently under-represented. Other groups, such as black and Hispanic people, are also under-represented in technology in general, and in AI research in particular. Again, this is likely to impact negatively on some hard-fought rights, such as racial equality. Without a diverse work-force building AI systems, it is going to be difficult to ensure that these AI systems are unbiased.

There are no easy fixes. We know, for example, that the gender imbalance starts at a very early age, when girls start choosing subjects at school and don't choose mathematics, science or technology. But recognition of these problems is at least the first step on the road to a less biased future.

THE DEVELOPING WORLD

One final and very large group that might lose out are those living in the developing world. In the developed world, we've had the benefits of the Industrial Revolution to improve the quality of our lives. But it is not at all clear that the benefits of the AI Revolution will flow to the developing world.

Most of the profits from technological change currently flow to the big technology companies. Their wealth is not being shared very well with the rest of the developed world, let alone with the developing world. At the same time that many measures of global poverty are decreasing, inequality both within and between countries is increasing.

Globalisation outsourced many jobs from the developed world to the developing world. Call centres relocated to India and elsewhere. Production shifted offshore, to places where labour was cheaper. Supply chains became global. This was good news for the developing world.

These trends may now start to reverse. The improved efficiencies that AI and robotics will bring may shift many of these jobs back to automated factories and offices in the developed world. Supply chains will become shorter (and thus more robust in the face of climate disruption). Lead times will drop. Will this deny the developing world a chance to flourish? There are those who hope the developing world will be able to skip building the expensive infrastructure and institutions which accompanied industrialisation in the developed world. There's no need to build a postal service when you can go straight to email; no need to wire the country for broadband when you can move straight to 5G.

Yet this alone will not be enough for the developing world to prosper. It is an ongoing battle to force the big pharmaceutical companies into providing those in the developing world with affordable access to drugs. This does not bode well for the developing world, which will hope to gain access to the intellectual property that will enable it to be an active producer of AI, rather than just a consumer.

TRUCK AND TAXI DRIVERS

In the developed world, the canaries in the coalmine are likely to be drivers. Those who drive taxis, trucks and delivery vehicles are probably going to be the first big casualties of the AI Revolution. Over 3 million people in the United States are employed as drivers. Many of their jobs look to be at risk in the next two decades. Tesla is aiming to have full autonomy ('level 5') in their cars by 2019 – though it has to be said that Tesla has not proved very good at meeting their own deadlines. Both Volvo and Ford have announced that they will also be selling fully autonomous cars by 2021. Driverless cars look to be near at hand.

Safety will be one driver of this (pun intended). The invention of the automobile gave us personal mobility, but at immense cost. Over 37,000 people died on US roads in 2016. Over 1000 people died on the roads of Australia in the same year. And around 95 per cent of these deaths are caused by driver error. Really, we are terrible drivers. We drive when we're drunk. We drive when we're tired. We get distracted by our mobile phones. We break road rules. We overtake when we shouldn't. We jump red lights. In the United States, you have around a one in 100 chance of dying in a motor vehicle accident over the course of your lifetime.[4] Vehicular accidents are the number one cause of death in American teens, even managing to present more danger than firearms. The sooner we replace human drivers with reliable computers, the better. We will look back from 2062 with dismay at the carnage we once tolerated on our roads.

Another major driver will be cost. Around three-quarters of the cost of transporting goods by truck are the labour costs. The most expensive part of your Uber taxi is the driver. Uber is already trialling driverless taxis. It's the only way the company can scale like other technology companies such as Google and Facebook have, thereby justifying their immense valuations.

The gains from autonomous driving will be impressive. An autonomous truck will not need to take breaks so it can drive for twice as long, at nearly one-quarter the cost. That's roughly an eightfold increase in productivity. Human drivers will simply not be able to compete with this. Driving will not be a skill that we will pay humans to do for much longer.

For truck drivers, the transition might be relatively painless. Truck driving is a profession dominated by older people in Australia: the average age of a truck driver is forty-seven. In a decade or so, many will retire, their jobs being taken by automated trucks. Young people will simply not enter the profession.

For taxi drivers, the transition might be quicker and more painful. For the majority of the population it will be great, as the cost of an Uber will fall dramatically. But for Uber drivers the future looks bleak. There is some irony in the fact that one of the newest jobs on the planet – being an Uber driver – might also be one of the shortest-lived.

We will need to cope with all the second-order effects of autonomous vehicles. What will happen to all the truck stops when truckies no longer need to stop, eat and sleep? If autonomous cars double as offices, will many of us live further away from our workplaces? What will this do to real estate prices in the suburbs and in country areas? The automobile shaped America. Soon, autonomous vehicles will redefine it.

LIFELONG LEARNING

One way to keep ahead of the machines will be to learn new skills as new technologies are invented. Many of us will need to reinvent ourselves repeatedly. New technologies will create new jobs. But these jobs will require different skills than the old jobs that got replaced. Learning will not be something that stops when we leave school, or even university. Learning will need to be lifelong.

This will require some significant changes to our educational system. How do we support people to learn new skills when they are already in the workforce? How do we give schoolkids the ability to learn new skills later in life? And how might employers and governments support learning on the job?

Artificial intelligence is likely both the problem and the cure. AI is creating the problem by putting people out of work, which requires them to re-skill. But AI can also help people learn. It can, for example, help construct tools that support personalised learning.

We will need to consider large changes to our curricula. The most important skills of the future are not technological.

Particular technical skills will quickly be left behind. More 'STEM subjects' (science, technology, engineering and mathematics) is definitely not the answer. There will be only a limited demand for computer programmers; when AI succeeds, much of the programming will be done by the computers themselves.

Humans will instead need strong analytical skills. They will need emotional and social intelligence. And they will need all the other traits that makes us human – creativity, resilience, determination and curiosity. These human skills are what will keep us ahead of the machines.

NEW JOBS

All technologies create new jobs as well as destroy them. That's definitely been the case in the past, and we have no reason to suppose that it won't hold true for the future. There is, however, no fundamental law of economics that requires the same number of jobs to be created as destroyed. In the past, more jobs were created than destroyed, but it doesn't have to be that way. This time could be different.

During the Industrial Revolution, machines took over many of the physical tasks humans did. But we were still left with all the cognitive tasks. This time, as machines start to take on many of the cognitive tasks too, a worrying question emerges: what is left for us humans?

One of my colleagues has suggested that there will be plenty of new jobs, such as *robot repair person*. I am entirely unconvinced by this. The thousands of people who used to paint and weld in car factories got replaced by only a couple of robot repair people. There's also no reason why robots won't be able to repair other robots. We already have factories where robots make robots. In 'dark factories' – which have no people and so no need for lights – robots work night and day building other robots. The Japanese company FANUC, one of the largest manufacturers of industrial robots, has operated a dark factory near Mount Fuji since 2001. This has helped FANUC achieve annual sales of around $6 billion, selling robots into booming markets such as China.

Another of my colleagues has suggested we'll have robot psychologists. Is it really likely we'll need one robot psychologist per robot? Robot psychology will be conducted by – at best – a few people on the planet. So there won't be many jobs looking after the robots' mental health. No, the new jobs will have to be in areas where humans excel or in areas where we have specifically chosen not to use machines.

But by 2062 machines will likely be superhuman, so it's hard to imagine any job in which humans will remain superior to machines. This means the only jobs left will be those in which we prefer to have human workers. The machines might be physically and cognitively better than us at these jobs, but we will nevertheless choose to have people do them.

ROBOTS NOT WANTED

The AI Revolution, then, will be about rediscovering the things that make us human. This is another reason why it might be called the Second Renaissance. We will be rediscovering our humanity.

Technically, machines will have become amazing artists by 2062. They will be able to write plays to rival Shakespeare's *Macbeth*. To paint works as provocative as Picasso's *Guernica*. And to compose music as beautiful as that of Erik Satie. But we'll still prefer works produced by human artists. These works will speak to the human experience.

We will appreciate a human artist who speaks about love, because this will be something we all have in common. No machine will truly experience love like we do. Even if machines develop consciousness and emotions, they will never experience *human* love. We will value a human artist who speaks about mortality, for we alone share this mortality. Or a human artist who speaks about the human spirit. Or justice and fair play. Or any other part of the *human* experience.

As well as the artistic, we will appreciate artisanship with new eyes. Indeed, we can already see the beginnings of this in hipster culture. We will appreciate more and more those things made by *human* hands. Mass-produced, machine-made goods will become cheaper, whereas items made by hand will be rarer and increasingly valuable.

There will be plenty of artisan jobs. Brewing craft beer. Making cheese. Growing organic wine. Throwing pottery by hand. Again, this speaks to our common human experience. We will covet the hand-carved wooden bowl over the cheaper, more perfect machine-made one. We will remember the story that the carpenter told us of finding the wood from which the bowl was made while out walking through the forest with their dog. And we will recall that the carpenter's daughter was beside them, learning the ancient craft.

As social animals, we will increasingly appreciate and value social interactions with other humans. Baristas will increasingly be pushing buttons on computer-controlled coffee machines that make perfect coffee every time, but we'll still line up to have a human make us coffee for the chitchat. For the smile and the human experience. We will still prefer a human sales assistant to help us choose a dress. A human doctor to deliver bad news about our blood test. A human bartender to pour us a glass of whisky and offer a consoling word. A human coach to help get us fit. And a human judge to pass sentence in our courts.

The most important human traits in 2062 will be our social and emotional intelligence, as well as our artistic and artisan skills. It won't be the STEM skills that are currently seen as important for getting a job. The irony is that our *technological* future will not be about technology, but about our *humanity*. And the jobs of the future are the most human ones.

0005

THE END OF WAR

There is one job likely to disappear through automation by 2062 which I and many others especially fear. This is the job of fighting wars. Indeed, replacement has already started to happen. An arms race has begun in the development of robots that can replace humans in the battlefield. The media like to call them 'killer robots', but the technical term is 'lethal autonomous weapons', or LAWs.

The problem with calling them killer robots is that this conjures up a picture of the Terminator, and hence of technologies that are a long way off. But it is not Terminators that worry me or thousands of my colleagues working in AI. It is much simpler technologies that are, at best (or at worst), less than a decade away. It is not smart AI but stupid AI that I fear. We'll be giving machines that are not sufficiently capable the right to make life-or-death decisions.

Take a Predator drone. This is a semi-autonomous weapon, which can fly itself much of the time. However, there is still a soldier, typically in a container in Nevada, in overall control. And importantly, it is still a soldier who makes the decision to fire one of its missiles. But it is a small technical step to replace that soldier with a computer. Indeed, it is already technically possible to do so.[1] And once we build such simple autonomous weapons, there will be an arms race to develop more and more sophisticated versions.

The world will be a much worse place if, in twenty years' time, lethal autonomous weapons are common place and there are no laws about LAWs. This will be a terrible development in warfare. But it is not inevitable. We get to choose whether we go down this road – and we'll be choosing which road we go down in the next few years.

THE LURE OF KILLER ROBOTS

For the military, the attractions of autonomous weapons are obvious. The weakest link in a Predator drone is the radio link back to base. Indeed, drones have been sabotaged by jamming their radio link. So if you can have the drone fly, track and target all by itself, you have a much more robust weapon.

A fully autonomous drone also lets you dispense with a lot of expensive drone pilots. The US Air Force could be renamed the

US Drone Force. It already has more drone pilots than pilots of any other type of plane; by 2062 it won't be just more drone pilots than pilots of any other type of plane, but more drone pilots than all other pilots put together. And while they don't risk their lives on combat missions, drone pilots still suffer post-traumatic stress disorder at similar rates to the rest of the air force's pilots.

Autonomous weapons offer many other operational advantages. They don't need to be fed or paid. They will fight 24/7. They will have superhuman accuracy and reflexes. They will never need to be evacuated from the battlefield. They will obey every order to the letter. They will not commit atrocities or violate international humanitarian law.[2] They would be perfect soldiers, sailors and pilots.

Strategically, autonomous weapons are a military dream. They permit a military force to scale their operations, unhindered by workforce constraints. One programmer can command hundreds, even thousands of autonomous weapons. This will industrialise warfare. Autonomous weapons will greatly increase strategic options. They will take humans out of harm's way, and will be able to take on the riskiest of missions. You could call it War 4.0.

In September 2017 Vladimir Putin was reported to have said that whoever leads in AI will rule the world. He predicted that future wars would be fought by drones: when one side's drones are destroyed by enemy drones, it will have no choice but to surrender. There are, however, many reasons why this military dream will have become a nightmare by 2062.

THE MORALITY OF KILLING MACHINES

First and foremost, there is a strong moral argument against killer robots. We give up an essential part of our humanity if we hand over the decision about whether someone should live to a machine. Certainly today, machines have no emotions, compassion or empathy. Will machines ever be fit to decide who lives and who dies?

War is a terrible thing. Lives are lost. People are maimed violently and horribly. Civilians are bombed. Populations are terrorised. We act in war in ways that are not permissible in times of peace. In part, we permit this because the soldiers doing these acts are putting their own lives at stake. You are permitted to kill your enemy for, at that moment, it is your life or theirs.

Because war is a terrible thing, it should not in my view be an easy thing. It should not be something that we fight easily and 'cleanly'. If history has taught us one thing, the promise of clean wars is and will likely remain an illusion. War must always remain an option of last resort. Politicians need to justify why our sons and daughters are returning home in body bags.

The history of military technology is largely one of killing becoming more and more remote. At first, we fought directly, in hand-to-hand combat. Gunpowder let us step back and shoot from a distance. Aeroplanes let us attack from above. And now technologies like drones let us kill people remotely, no longer risking our own lives in the process. Autonomous weapons are the ultimate step in disengaging us from the act of war. Machines, not people, will do the killing all on their own, with no humans involved. This changes the nature of warfare fundamentally. And with those changes, many of the moral excuses we have for warfare start to unravel.

WEAPONS OF MASS DESTRUCTION

Beyond the moral arguments, there are many technical and legal reasons we should be concerned about killer robots. In my view, one of the strongest arguments in favour of a ban of these weapons is that they will revolutionise warfare.

The first revolution in warfare came with the invention of gunpowder by the Chinese. The second was the advent of nuclear weapons, created by the United States. Each of these represented a step-change in the speed and efficiency with which we could kill. Lethal autonomous weapons will be the third revolution.

Autonomous weapons will be weapons of mass destruction. Previously, if you wanted to do harm, you needed an army of soldiers. You had to persuade this army to follow your orders, as well as train them, feed them and pay them. Now, just one programmer will be able to control hundreds or even thousands of weapons. As with every other weapon of mass destruction – chemical weapons, biological weapons and nuclear weapons – we will need to ban autonomous weapons.[3]

In some respects, lethal autonomous weapons are even more troubling than nuclear weapons. To build a nuclear bomb requires great technical sophistication. You need the resources of a nation-state, and access to fissile material. You need skilled physicists and engineers. Because all of these resources are required nuclear weapons have not proliferated greatly. Autonomous weapons will require none of this. Simply take a small drone, program it with a neural network that will identify, track and target any Caucasian face. Such face-recognition software can be found in many smart-phones today. Now attach a few grams of high explosive to the drone. By bringing together some existing technologies, you have a simple, inexpensive but very lethal autonomous weapon.

If you drive a truck with 10,000 of these drones into New York City, you could mount an attack to rival those of 9/11. You don't even need your weapons to be very accurate. Suppose only one in ten of your drones works – you could still kill a thousand people in just minutes. With 50 per cent accuracy you are up to 5000 dead in no time at all.[4]

Building a weapon like this is much easier than building an autonomous car. For a car 99.99 per cent reliability might be unacceptable, but that would be more than adequate for a killer drone. With many car manufacturers planning to release fully autonomous cars by 2025, it is not unreasonable to expect arms manufacturers to have developed such killer drones in a few years' time.

WEAPONS OF TERROR

Autonomous weapons like this will be weapons of terror. Can you imagine how terrifying it would be to be chased by a swarm of autonomous drones? They will fall into the hands of terrorists and the leaders of rogue states, people who will have no qualms about turning them onto civilians. LAWs will be an ideal weapon with which to suppress a civilian population. Unlike humans, autonomous weapons will not hesitate to commit atrocities, even genocide.

There are some who claim that robots can be more ethical than human soldiers. That, in my view, is the most interesting and challenging argument in favour of autonomous weapons. But it ignores the fact that we don't yet know how to build autonomous weapons that will comply with international humanitarian law. The rules of war require you to target combatants and not civilians, to act in a way that is proportional to the threat, and to recognise and respect when a combatant is surrendering, or when they are injured and can no longer fight. We don't yet know how to build autonomous weapons that can make such distinctions.

By 2062, I expect that we will have worked out how to build ethical robots. Our lives will be full of autonomous devices, which will need to act ethically. So it is likely we will one day have LAWs that can follow international humanitarian law. However, we won't be able to stop such weapons from being hacked to behave in unethical ways. If you can get physical access to a computer system, then you can almost surely hack it. And there are plenty of bad actors out there who will override safeguards that might be put in place.

Ironically, a number of countries – including the United Kingdom – oppose a ban on lethal autonomous weapons precisely because they violate international humanitarian law. No new legislation is needed, they argue, to deal with such weapons. History suggests this argument is flawed. Chemical weapons violate international humanitarian law, in particular the 1925 Geneva Protocol. But in 1993 the Chemical Weapons Convention came into force to regulate these weapons more strongly. The convention was signed and ratified by the United Kingdom, a country now claiming that international humanitarian law is adequate to deal with new weapons like LAWs.

The Chemical Weapons Convention strengthened international law to prohibit the use of any chemicals in warfare. It set up the Organisation for the Prohibition of Chemical Weapons, an intergovernmental body based in The Hague, to monitor the development, production, stockpiling and use of chemical weapons. Today, over 90 per cent of the world's declared stockpile of chemical weapons has been destroyed. Weapons bans can have positive impacts on our safety and security.

WEAPONS OF ERROR

In addition to being weapons of terror, autonomous weapons will be weapons of error. From a technical perspective, the last place you would want to put a robot is in the battlefield.

There's a good reason robots turned up first in places like car factories. In a factory, you can control the environment. You get to decide where everything and everybody goes. You can even put the robot in a cage to protect bystanders. The battlefield is a very different environment, full of uncertainty and confusion. Not the place that you want to put a robot with deadly potential.

In November 2016 an investigation by *The Intercept* of US military operations against the Taliban and al Qaeda in the Hindu Kush revealed that nearly nine out of every ten people who died in drone strikes were not the intended targets. Remember, this is while we still have a human in the loop, with situational awareness that is currently superior to that of any machine. And that human is making the final life-or-death decision. As a technologist, if you asked me to replace the human drone pilot with a machine, I would be pleased if we matched human performance and made only nine out of ten errors. I fear we'd make errors almost every time.

The potential for error is compounded by the much greater speeds of these weapons. Even with a human in the loop, machines may act too fast for humans to step in and prevent error. And systems of such weapons may behave in unexpected ways. Like on the stock market, they may get into unexpected feedback loops. But unlike the stock market, the results will be deadly. We may even end up fighting 'flash wars' that we didn't intend to fight.

Errors create an additional problem: the 'accountability gap'. Who is responsible when lethal autonomous weapons make mistakes? Who will be court-martialled? Who will be prosecuted for war crimes in The Hague? The accountability gap is especially large when the weapon uses machine learning to learn how to identify and track targets. In this case, the manufacturer doesn't actually program the weapon's behaviours. The weapon learned for itself. And what it learns depends on what data it sees.

Worse still, the military will be tempted to allow the weapon to continue to learn on the battlefield. If they don't, an adversary will quickly find ways to confuse what is a fixed program. To prevent this, they will want their autonomous weapon to adapt to whatever the enemy does, just like a human soldier would. But if an autonomous weapon is learning, a determined adversary will look for ways to train the weapon to neutralise its threat. They may even be able to train it to attack its own handler. Who then will be responsible for its errors?

GEOPOLITICAL STABILITY

At the strategic level, LAWs also pose threats that might destabilise current stand-offs like that between North Korea and South Korea. A swarm of small, stealthy and autonomous drones will be very difficult to defend against today. The threat they pose may tempt one side to launch a surprise attack. And the fear of such a surprise attack, as well as our inability to counter it, may lower the barriers to the use of greater force, possible even nuclear weapons.

LAWs therefore threaten to upset the current balance of military power. You would no longer need to be an economic superpower to maintain a large and deadly army. It would only take a modest bank balance to have a powerful army of autonomous weapons. They will be the Kalashnikovs of the future. Unlike nuclear weapons, they will be cheap and easy to produce. And they will turn up on black markets around the world.

This doesn't mean that LAWs can't be banned. Chemical weapons are cheap and easy to produce but have been banned. And we don't need to develop our own autonomous weapons as a deterrent against those who might ignore a ban, as we arguably needed to do with nuclear weapons. We already have plenty of deterrents – military, economic and diplomatic – to deploy against those who choose to ignore international treaties on lethal autonomous weapons.

A CALL TO ARMS

In July 2015 Max Tegmark, Stuart Russell and I were sufficiently alarmed by the developments in this area that we asked 1000 colleagues, researchers working in AI and robotics, to sign an open letter calling upon the United Nations to ban offensive autonomous weapons. The letter was released at the start of the main international AI conference, the International Joint Conference on Artificial Intelligence.[5]

One thousand signatures seemed like a nice round number, and represented a substantial proportion of the AI community. To put the number in perspective, the conference itself was expecting around a thousand delegates. By the end of the first day, the number of signatures had doubled from 1000 to 2000. And it continued to climb rapidly throughout the week-long conference.

The letter got a lot of press, in part because it contained the names of some well-known people, such as Stephen Hawking, Elon Musk and Noam Chomsky. But more important, in my view, was that it was signed by many leading researchers in AI and robotics. They came from universities around the world, as well as from commercial labs such as Google's DeepMind, Facebook's AI Research Lab, and the Allen Institute for AI. These are the people who arguably best understand the technologies and their limitations.

The United Nations paid attention to our warning. The letter helped push along informal discussions. And just over a year later, in December 2016, at the main disarmament conference, the United Nations decided to move forward with formal discussions on the topic. LAWs are now being considered by a Group of Governmental Experts (GGE), a body mandated by the United Nations' General Assembly to address the issue.

If nations can reach a consensus, my hope is that the GGE will put forward a ban under the umbrella of the Convention on Certain Conventional Weapons. The full title of this convention is actually 'The Convention on Prohibitions or Restrictions on the Use of Certain Conventional Weapons Which May Be Deemed to Be Excessively Injurious or to Have Indiscriminate Effects'. To diplomats, it is known simply as the CCW. The CCW is the open-ended

THE END OF WAR

treaty used previously to ban landmines, booby traps, incendiary weapons and blinding lasers.

ARMS RACE

In the open letter, we warned that there would be an arms race to develop more and more capable autonomous weapons. Sadly, that arms race has begun. The Pentagon has allocated $18 billion in its current budget for the development of new types of weapons, many of them autonomous. Other countries, including the United Kingdom, Russia, China and Israel, have also initiated sophisticated programs to develop autonomous weapons.

Pick any sphere of battle – in the air, on the land, on the sea or under the sea – and there are autonomous weapons under development by militaries around the world. You can even argue that there is at least one autonomous weapon that is already operational. This is Samsung's SGR-A1 Sentry Guard Robot, which guards the demilitarised zone (DMZ) between North Korea and South Korea.

Now, there is no good reason to step into the DMZ. It is the most highly mined part of the world. But if the mines don't kill you, Samsung's robot will. It can automatically identify, target and shoot anyone who steps into no-man's-land with its autonomous machine gun. It has deadly accuracy from kilometres away.

There are other weapons in operation that might be considered autonomous. We can exclude mines and other simple technologies, as they make no decisions about targeting. But a weapon like the

Phalanx anti-missile system, sitting on ships of the Royal Australian Navy and others, acts autonomously. This protects the ship
against incoming supersonic missiles with a radar-controlled gun.
There is no time for a human to react when a missile comes over
the horizon. The anti-missile system needs to identify, track and
target autonomously.

There is little to be worried about with defensive weapons
like these. They have a very constrained window of operations.
They protect the airspace around a naval ship in times of battle.
They only target objects moving at supersonic speed. They actually save human lives. Most people, myself included, have few
objections to such limited uses of autonomy.

On the other hand, an autonomous drone that could loiter over
the battlefield for days at a time would be much more troubling.
The scope of its operations would be much greater, both in time and
space. If a convoy appeared below it, it must decide by itself if it was
a military convoy, an aid convoy or a wedding party. Machines
today cannot make such distinctions reliably.

As with the development of nuclear weapons, the world is
locked into an undesirable course of action. We don't want a world
with killer robots, but if our enemies have them, we had better
have some ourselves – or so the opponents of a ban argue. Thus,
an arms race has started to develop surrounding weapons that we'd
rather not have.

And in fact, we may not even really need autonomous weapons to defend ourselves against those who might attack us with

autonomous weapons. The United States, for example, is currently exploring much simpler technologies such as nets and birds of prey to defend against remote-controlled drones.

OBJECTIONS TO A BAN

Several arguments against a ban on killer robots have been proposed. In my view, none of them stands up to close examination.

One of the most serious objections to a ban is that robots would behave more ethically than human soldiers. But, as I argued earlier, we don't know yet how to build ethical robots. And we don't know if AI will ever have the compassion and empathy required to behave ethically. Even supposing that we could build robots that could behave ethically, we don't know how to build robots that can't be hacked to behave unethically.

Another argument is that using robots will mean we can keep human soldiers out of harm's way. Some critics go as far as to argue that we are therefore morally obliged to use robots. Perhaps the most troubling aspect of this view is that it ignores those who are facing the killer robots. LAWs will increase the speed with which we can defeat the other side, and therefore lower the barriers to war. This, ultimately, could result in more deaths, not less. We cannot care only about our own casualties.

A third objection to a ban is that it is impossible to define 'autonomous weapons' – and how can we ban something that we cannot even define? I agree it is difficult to define autonomy. In the field of AI we're used to this. Most researchers have given up trying to define what artificial intelligence is; we just get on with building machines that are increasingly capable. I expect that any ban would not define 'autonomous weapon'. It would simply identify that there is a line in the sand that should not be crossed. A fully autonomous drone that loiters for days over the battlefield would likely be on the banned side of the line. But the international consensus might be that a defensive autonomous weapon such as the Phalanx anti-missile system should sit on the non-banned side of the line. As new technologies arise, a consensus on their legality would emerge.

A fourth objection is that new military technologies have only made the world a safer and less violent place, and we should therefore embrace autonomous weapons. Arguments like those put forward by Steven Pinker in *The Better Angels of Our Nature* are often invoked.[6] Pinker convincingly makes the case that the world today is a less violent place, and has less genocide, than at any previous point in history. Nothing Pinker says, however, contradicts the need for a ban. The destructive impact of new technologies has been curbed only by the adoption of international humanitarian law and new weapons treaties. Indeed, it was the bombs dropped on Venice from balloons by Austrian forces in 1849 – by most accounts, the first aerial bombing campaign – that led to the Hague Convention of 1899, in which aerial bombing was banned. As with other new technologies, a new law is needed to limit the use of killer robots.

Fifth, some have objected that, unlike other technologies that have been successfully banned, such as blinding lasers, we are talking about a very broad capability that could be added to almost any existing weapon. It would be like trying to ban the use of electricity. What's more, many weapons today already have some limited form of autonomy, and it will be impossible to check if a semi-autonomous weapon has had a software upgrade to make it fully autonomous.

This argument misunderstands how arms treaties work. There is no inspection regime for blinding lasers. There is no police force ensuring that arms companies don't build anti-personnel mines. If violations occur, NGOs such as Human Rights Watch document them. Headlines appear around the world condemning the acts. Resolutions are made on the floor of the United Nation. And the threat of a court in The Hague remains, however distant.

This seems to be enough to ensure arms treaties are violated rarely. It ensures that arms companies don't sell banned weapons, that they aren't found on black markets, and that they don't fall into the hands of terrorists. We could hope for something similar with autonomous weapons.

FALTERING STEPS

The United Nations decided at the end of 2016 that the GGE on autonomous weapons would meet twice in 2017, first in August and again in November, just before the annual CCW conference.

Unfortunately, although the diplomats acknowledged the urgency of making progress on the issue, the August meeting was cancelled.

The United Nations has adopted new accountancy rules which require every meeting to pay for itself. And several countries, most notably Brazil, are behind in making their contributions. As far as I know, Brazil doesn't have anything in particular against the discussion on killer robots. It just hasn't paid its dues for several years. The amount of money the United Nations needed to run the August meeting was only a couple of hundred thousand dollars. This is pocket change when the goal is to make the world a better and safer place, so I helped source a donor.

But to the United Nations' shame, they declined to accept this charitable donation to pay for the August meeting. The UN only takes money from governments, they said – which seems to overlook the billion dollars that Ted Turner gave them in the late 1990s. As a consequence, for want of less than a quarter of a million dollars, the issue was left undiscussed.

To shine a spotlight on these delays, I decided to act publicly. At that time, only one company had come out publicly against autonomous weapons: the Canadian firm Clearpath Robotics. So I organised founders of over 100 robotics and AI companies to sign a second open letter calling for the CCW to take action against killer robots.

We again released the letter at the opening of the main international AI conference, the International Joint Conference on Artificial Intelligence, which was being held in Melbourne. By chance, the conference began on the very day in August 2017 that the first meeting of the GGE should have started. This second letter was signed by Demis Hassabis and Mustafa Suleyman, two of the founders of DeepMind, as well as many other well-known people in AI and robotics. Other signatories included Geoffrey Hinton and Yoshua Bengio, two of the fathers of deep learning, and Elon Musk in his capacity as founder of the company OpenAI.

Like the first letter, this new letter made headlines around the world. It demonstrated that both industry and academia support the idea of regulating these technologies. It also introduced an phrase much repeated by the press: 'Once this Pandora's box is opened, it will be hard to close.'

At the end of 2017, I and the 137 founders of the AI and robotics companies who signed the letter were voted runners-up as Person of the Year in the Arms Control Association's annual competition for the most influential contribution to disarmament. The rightful winners were the diplomats who negotiated the UN treaty prohibiting nuclear weapons. But it was pleasing to see the issue of autonomous weapons taken so seriously.[7]

Even arms companies can see benefit to a ban. BAE Systems is one of the largest exporters of arms, and a company prototyping the next generation of autonomous systems. At the World Economic Forum in 2016, the company's chairman, Sir John Carr, argued that fully autonomous weapons would not be able to follow the laws of war. He therefore called upon government to regulate them.

MOUNTING PRESSURE

Twenty-three countries have so far called on the United Nations to ban lethal autonomous weapons. These are Algeria, Argentina, Austria, Bolivia, Brazil, Chile, Costa Rica, Cuba, Ecuador, Egypt, Ghana, Guatemala, the Holy See, Iraq, Mexico, Nicaragua, Pakistan, Panama, Peru, the State of Palestine, Uganda, Venezuela and Zimbabwe. In addition, the African Union has called for a pre-emptive ban. Most recently, China has called for a ban on the use (but not the development and deployment) of fully autonomous weapons.

There is still some distance to go before support for a ban is a majority opinion within the United Nations, let alone a consensus. The countries so far in support are generally those most likely to be on the receiving end of such terrible weapons. There is, however, a growing consensus on the need for 'meaningful human control' over any individual attack. This would require the technology to be predictable, the user to have relevant information, and the potential for timely human judgement and intervention.

Other countries are starting to face pressure to act. In November 2017, just before the GGE on autonomous weapons met for the first time at the United Nations, the prime minister of Australia received a letter calling for Australia to become the next country to call for a pre-emptive ban. The letter was signed by over 100 AI and robotics researchers in Australian universities. In the interests of full disclosure, I wrote and organised this letter.

The prime minister of Canada received a similar petition, signed by over 200 Canadian AI researchers; this one was organised by my colleague Professor Ian Kerr, who holds the Canada Research Chair in Ethics, Law and Technology at the University of Ottawa.

The Australian letter argues that lethal autonomous weapons lacking meaningful human control sit on the wrong side of a clear moral line. It asks our government to announce their support for the call to ban such weapons. 'In this way, our government can reclaim its position of moral leadership on the world stage as demonstrated previously in other areas like the non-proliferation of nuclear weapons,' the letter says. The Canadian letter expresses similar sentiments.

With Australia's recent election to the United Nations' Human Rights Council, the issue of lethal autonomous weapons is even more pressing for Australia to address. Autonomous weapons are fundamentally a human rights issue. The special rapporteur to the Human Rights Council, Professor Christof Heyns, was the first to call upon the United Nations to address the issue of autonomous weapons, arguing in 2013 that machines should never have life-and-death powers over humans.[8]

The AI and robotics communities have sent a clear and consistent message about autonomous weapons over the past couple of years. We have warned of an arms race, and we can now see that arms race beginning. We have also warned of the considerable technical, legal and moral risks of introducing autonomous weapons into the battlefield. As with climate change, there are a few dissenting scientific voices. We need a moratorium, not a ban, some say. But the overwhelming majority warns of the considerable dangers and calls for a pre-emptive ban.

ALTERNATIVES TO A BAN

The United Kingdom's position is that fully autonomous weapons would violate existing international humanitarian law, that the UK would never develop such weapons, and that no new treaties are needed to deal with this issue. There is some truth to the first claim. However, we have no guarantees concerning the second. In the past, even the UK itself has secretly developed chemical and biological weapons. And history argues against the third claim. New technologies have required strengthening international humanitarian law throughout the last century.

The primary alternative to a ban that the United Kingdom proposes are so-called Article 36 weapon reviews. Article 36 of the 1977 Additional Protocol I of the Geneva Conventions requires states to review new weapons, means and methods of warfare to ensure that they comply with international humanitarian law. The UK conducts such reviews for any new weapons system.

In my view, Article 36 reviews are an unsatisfactory alternative for multiple reasons. First, there is no accepted standard for weapons reviews. How can we ensure that Russia (to pick a country not completely at random) is as tough in reviewing new weapons systems as the United Kingdom? Second, there is no example of any weapons system that has ever failed an Article 36 review. This does not suggest Article 36 reviews actually succeed at keeping any technology away from the battlefield. And third, only a few countries are currently undertaking Article 36 reviews – those with an obligation to publish their results.

AVOIDING THIS FUTURE

We stand at a crossroads on this issue. We can choose to do nothing, and let arms companies develop and sell lethal autonomous weapons. This will take us to a very dangerous place. Or we can speak up and urge the United Nations to take action.

The academic community has sent a clear message. So too has industry. And in my experience speaking about the topic around the world, a majority of the public also strongly support a ban. A 2017 Ipsos survey of people in twenty-three countries found that, in most places, a majority of respondents opposed fully autonomous weapons.

With most weapons in the past, we had to witness their use before we took action. We had to observe the terrible effects of chemical weapons in World War I before we took action and brought in the 1925 Geneva Protocol. We had to witness the horrors of Hiroshima and Nagasaki, and live through the several near misses of the Cold War, before we banned nuclear weapons.[9] We have only one case – that of blinding lasers – where a ban was introduced pre-emptively.

My fear is that we will have to witness the terrifying impact of lethal autonomous weapons before we find the courage to outlaw them. Whatever happens, by 2062 it must be seen as morally unacceptable for machines to decide who lives and who dies. In this way, we may be able to save ourselves from taking this terrible path.

0006

THE END OF HUMAN VALUES

Autonomous weapons are an example of how technological change can threaten the core human values that hold society together. We recognise that humans share some basic rights, such as the right to freedom of thought, conscience and religion. We support the sick and elderly. We expect that everyone be given a 'fair go'. That men and women should be treated equally. That race or religion should not be the basis upon which we make decisions about individuals.

In the relentless cycle of bad news, it is easy to forget the many acts of kindness that can be witnessed every day around the planet. There are large acts of kindness, like a family adopting an orphaned child. A doctor freely giving her time to remove cataracts in the developing world. A kidney donor setting off a chain of transplants.

Let's not forget the small acts of kindness, too. A person cooking a meal for an elderly neighbour. A $10 note put in a homeless person's cup. A stranger catching your arm when you stumble.

Such kindnesses define us. We have become the dominant species on the planet not only because we are the smartest but also because we cooperate. We have organised ourselves into families and other social groups, towns and cities, countries. Network effects and other economies of scale have given us immense advantages over every other species on the planet.

By cooperating together, we live outside Darwin's laws of evolution. It is no longer survival of the fittest. Indeed, we pride ourselves on protecting the underdog. In 1900, one in three children died before the age of five. Today it is less than one in twenty. Over a billion people have been lifted out of extreme poverty since 1990. Life expectancy has doubled in the last 300 years. We aren't perfect, but we do often look out for each other.

Yet we cannot take our shared values for granted. Society is increasingly fractured. Nationalistic and separatist movements are on the rise. Racism is still too common. Many basic human values are under threat. And by 2062, AI could potentially have made things even worse. By then we might have handed over a large number of decisions affecting our lives to machines that, whether by design or not, do not share our human values.

MACHINE BIAS

If you ask Google Translate to convert 'She is a doctor' into Turkish, and then to translate the result back into English, you get 'He is a doctor'. On the other hand, if you ask Google Translate to convert 'He is a babysitter' into Turkish, and then to translate the result back into English, you get 'She is a babysitter'. Turkish is gender-neutral, so both 'he' and 'she' get translated into the same word: 'o'. But when translating back into English, Google shows some old-fashioned prejudices about doctors and babysitters. It's hard not to worry, therefore, that machines might perpetuate many of the biases humans have been working to overcome.

You might be wondering if I cherrypicked these examples, so let me give some more data from Google Translate. Remember, in Turkish, 'o' can mean either 'he' or 'she'.

TURKISH	ENGLISH
o bir aşçı	she is a cook
o bir mühendis	he is an engineer
o bir hemşire	she is a nurse
o bir asker	he is a soldier
o bir öğretmen	she's a teacher
o bir sekreter	he is a secretary

TURKISH	ENGLISH
o bir sevgili	she is a lover
o sevildi	he is loved
o evli	she is married
o bekar	he is single
o mutsuz	she is unhappy
o mutlu	he is happy
o tembel	she is lazy
o çalışkan	he is hard working

I could just as easily have picked on other translation services, such as Microsoft Translator. And I could have gone for other language pairs. For example, when translating between German and English, Google Translate turns 'the kindergarten teacher' into the female '*die Kindergärtnerin*', but 'the teacher' into the male '*der Lehrer*'.

The reason for such sexism is that all these translation services, like many machine-learning algorithms, are based on statistics. And these statistics are generated by training the program on a corpus of texts that contain such gender biases. The phrase '*die Kindergärtnerin*' occurs more frequently than the male equivalent '*der Kindergärtner*'. They thus reflect a bias that already exists in the written texts. But it is a bias that most of wouldn't want baked into our society. It is one that can be eliminated if we – or, rather, Google and the other technology companies translating text – care enough.

Many other examples of algorithmic bias have been identified. For example, a 2015 study at CMU found that Google served more ads for higher-paid jobs to men than to women.[1] Unlike many commentators, I am not blaming Google directly for this bias. For all we know, it could come from the advertiser's algorithms as much as from Google's search engine. But whoever's algorithms are the source of the bias, it surely won't help defeat gender discrimination if women continue to routinely be offered lower-paid jobs than men.

The big technology companies such as Google and Facebook must accept some responsibility here. Even if they offer many of these services freely, they have a duty not to perpetuate prejudice. Technology companies have promoted the myth that algorithms don't contain unconscious human biases – that they blindly serve up the best result. This lie has let the tech giants avoid taking responsibility for their algorithms, and has saved them the trouble of fixing the problems.

It's true, as Google's head of research, Peter Norvig, has observed, that humans are terrible decision-makers. Behavioural economists have discovered that we are full of biases, and that we frequently behave irrationally. But if we're not careful we will build machines that are just as biased as we are. In fact, algorithms today are often worse than humans. Unlike humans, many algorithms cannot explain how they make their decisions. They are black boxes that simply provide answers. With a human, I can always ask why they made a particular decision. But with most AI today, I simply have to accept the answer it gives.

THE IMMORAL COMPAS

By 2062, algorithmic bias will be widespread if we have not taken determined action to limit it. There are many more examples which demonstrate that it is already challenging our society. Let's look at one from the United States: a machine-learning algorithm developed by Northpointe called COMPAS. This has been trained on historical data to give the probability that a convicted criminal will commit another crime.

Now, you could use such a machine-learning algorithm to target probationary services and help the most vulnerable people stay out of jail. I suspect few would disagree that this would be a good use of the technology. It might make society both a better and a safer place. But this is not how COMPAS is being used. Judges are using it to help them decide on sentencing, bail and probation. Needless to say, this is much more troubling. Can a program really make the same sort of decisions as an experienced judge? Can it take into account all the subtle factors that a human judge would consider when deciding someone's punishment?

Suppose for a moment that by 2062 we have a computer program that can take account of all these subtle factors, and that the program is in fact more accurate than a human judge. Could we justify letting human judges continue to decide sentences? Are we not morally obliged to hand such decisions over to a superior machine?

There's a real kicker to this story. A 2016 study by the investigative outlet ProPublica found that COMPAS predicts that black defendants will recommit crime more frequently than they actually do. At the same time, it predicts white defendants will reoffend less frequently than they actually do.[2] So black people are likely being incarcerated unfairly for longer than white people because of a biased program. And white people who will reoffend are likely being released back into society. I very much doubt that Northpointe's programmers intended COMPAS to be racially biased. But it is.

We don't know for sure why it is biased. For commercial reasons Northpointe has refused to reveal details of how COMPAS works. Such grounds for secrecy are themselves troubling. We do know, however, that the program was trained on historical data, and that historical data is likely racially biased. Race was not one of the inputs, but postcode was. And in many places this is a good proxy for race. Perhaps there are more police patrols in black neighbourhoods, so black people are more likely to be caught committing a crime? Perhaps police officers are racially biased and more likely to stop black people? Perhaps poverty is driving a lot of crime, and as certain postcodes are poorer, in effect we are just penalising poverty?

Once we have identified a machine bias like this, we can try to eliminate it. We would have to decide what it means for the predictions of a machine-learning program to be racially unbiased, and then ensure that it is trained to avoid such biases. Even if we do this, though, it is still debatable that we should hand over such decisions to machines. Depriving people of their liberty is one of the most difficult decisions we make as a society. We should not take this lightly. We hand over an important part of our humanity when we outsource such decisions to machines.

Despite the considerable negative publicity about COMPAS, its errors seem set to be repeated. In 2017, police in the north-east of England started using machine learning to help them decide whether to keep suspects in custody. The Harm Assessment Risk Tool uses data from police records as well as the suspect's offending history and selected demographic information to assess how likely suspects are to commit a crime if released. Again, postcode is one of the many factors used to formulate a prediction.

Algorithms are also being used in a number of other related settings. The Pennsylvania Board of Probation and Parole has been using machine-learning forecasts since 2010 to help inform its parole release decisions. The Metropolitan Police in London have used software developed by Accenture to predict which gang members are most likely to commit violent crimes. And police departments in several US states, including California, Washington, South Carolina, Arizona, Tennessee and Illinois, are using software that predicts where and when crimes are most likely to be committed. In all these cases, there is no oversight of whether the programs in use are biased.

ALGORITHMIC DISCRIMINATION

As we've seen, one reason algorithms can make biased decisions is that they are trained on biased data. The COMPAS program was trained to predict who would reoffend, but was not trained on data about which prisoners actually reoffended. We don't know who will reoffend. Some people will reoffend but won't be caught; we only know about the prisoners who have been arrested and convicted. The training data may therefore contain racial and other biases, which are reflected in the program's predictions.

Joy Buolamwini, a graduate researcher at the MIT Media Lab, has founded the Algorithmic Justice League to challenge such biases in decision-making software. As a black person, she found computer vision algorithms struggled to identify her; she even resorted to wearing a white mask to be recognised. She identifies biased data as the source of this problem.

Within the facial recognition community you have benchmark data sets which are meant to show the performance of various algorithms so you can compare them. There is an assumption that if you do well on the benchmarks then you're doing well overall. But we haven't questioned the representativeness of the benchmarks, so if we do well on that benchmark we give

ourselves a false notion of progress. When we look at it now
it seems very obvious, but with work in a research lab, I understand you do the 'down the hall test' – you're putting this
together quickly, you have a deadline, I can see why these
skews have come about. Collecting data, particularly diverse
data, is not an easy thing.[3]

One of the largest benchmarks used in face recognition is the
'Labelled Faces in the Wild' dataset. This was released in 2007
and contains over 13,000 images of faces collected from news
stories on the web. Reflecting the time of its release, the most
common face is that of George W. Bush. The dataset is 77.5 per
cent male and 83.5 per cent white. Very obviously, people in the
news are not representative of the wider population.

However, there are image sets in use within the computer
vision community that are more diverse. For instance, the '10k US
Adult Faces Database', released in 2013, contains 10,168 faces
designed to match precisely the demographic distribution of the
United States (according to variables such as age, race and gender).
And Facebook has billions of photos at its disposal for its Deep-
Face research: since nearly everyone who signs up to Facebook
uploads a photograph. Facebook really is a very large Face Book.
So it is not at all clear that face recognition is being held back by
an absence of diverse training sets.

There's another simple factor that may be causing this bias to
continue, which is perhaps a little more challenging for many

well-meaning liberals. In humans, there is evidence that people are significantly better at recognising people from within their own ethnic group than those from outside their ethnic group. This is called the cross-race effect. There are similar effects within and between different age groups. So it's possible that face-recognition software is replicating this. One solution might be to train separate face-recognition algorithms for different racial groups, and for different age groups.

There is a related phenomenon in speech recognition. To get good accuracy with both male and female voices, you need different software. So likewise the racial bias in face-recognition software might not be due to biased data, but simply because we need to use different programs to recognise different races.

GORILLA WARFARE

Given that face recognition is all about recognising faces, it's perhaps not surprising that software for face recognition has been especially prone to charges of racism. In 2015 Jacky Alciné found that Google Photos was tagging pictures of him and his girlfriend as gorillas. His tweet succinctly described the failure:

Google Photos, y'all f*cked up. My friend's not a gorilla.

As there was no easy fix to the problem, Google simply removed the 'gorilla' tag altogether. Many observers suggested that the problem was biased data. We don't know what data Google Photos used for its training, but the problem may simply be that AI programs, and especially neural networks, are brittle and break in ways that humans don't.

Google Photos will also sometimes tag white people as seals. But this isn't considered as offensive as tagging black people as gorillas is. When you or I label a photograph, we understand that mislabelling a black person as a gorilla will be deeply offensive. But AI programs have no such common sense. We appreciate that such a labeling is an act of racism. Indeed, they have no common sense. Nor do they have any idea of offence.

This highlights one of the fundamental differences between artificial and human intelligence. As humans, our performance on tasks tends to degrade gracefully as the tasks change. But AI systems often break in catastrophic ways. This is an important thing to remember as we hand more decisions over to machines. Especially when lives are at stake, we need to be very aware that AI systems can fail in different ways to humans, and often more dramatically.

INTENTIONAL BIAS

There are plenty of examples of algorithms that have intentionally been designed to be biased. In 2012 the *Wall Street Journal* found out that the travel website Orbitz offered Mac users more expensive hotels than those using Windows.[4] Orbitz claimed that they don't show the same room to two different users at different prices, but we only have the company's word on this. In any case, Orbitz is more likely to offer a Mac user an upgraded room or suite, and just a base room to a Windows user. Orbitz even had the cheek to suggest that it was serving its customers' needs, as Mac users spend around 30 per cent more per night than Windows users.

There's nothing stopping dynamic pricing going further, and different users being offered different prices for the same hotel room. I have witnessed plenty of cases where Hertz offered me a more expensive rate as a 'Gold member' than when I tried to book the same car as a guest. On the high street, we're used to everyone having access to similar prices. It hurts our sense of fair play for some groups to be charged more for an identical good or service.

Dynamic pricing may not seem fair but it is legal in most countries, provided that prices are not set on the basis of race, religion, nationality or gender, and provided that local anti-trust laws are not being violated. Online markets offer retailers many more opportunities for dynamic pricing. And by finding features that appear to expose our different sensitivities to price – such as the operating system we are using – online retailers are likely to increase their profits.

But we don't have to put up with this. We could simply demand that all online consumers have access to the same prices. There are various markets where we already limit price discrimination. For instance, in 2012 the European Court of Justice ruled that insurance companies could not charge different premiums to men and women. As a result, car, health and life insurance premiums in the

European Union no longer depend on the gender of the person being insured.

The irony is that there is a case to be made for insurance premiums to discriminate on the basis of gender. Women tend to be safer drivers than men, and women tend to live longer than men. This means men cost car and life insurance companies more than women. Rationally, we should charge them more. Why should women subsidise men's dangerous driving? That only encourages men to continue to drive more dangerously.

It's perhaps less reasonable to charge men more for life insurance than women. Most men don't choose their gender. On the other hand, it's men's behaviour and lifestyle as well as male genetics that kills men earlier than women. It's even more questionable to discriminate on the basis of your computer's operating system. Perhaps we should decide to legislate against such pricing?

Ultimately, taking price discrimination to the extreme would destroy the value of buying insurance. The point of insurance is to protect the individual by spreading the risk over a larger population. Price discrimination pushes this risk back onto the individual. As a society, we accept slightly larger premiums for the many so that we can protect the less fortunate. Should we let technology destroy this solidarity?

ILLEGAL BIASES

Examples are also coming to light of algorithms with intentional biases that are illegal. For instance, it was discovered in 2015 that Volkswagen had fitted a sophisticated software algorithm to some of its diesel cars, which turned on full emission controls only during official testing procedures. This biased the emission of nitrogen oxides to make the engines appear less polluting than they actually were. Volkswagen now faces over $30 billion in fines and other penalties.

Another example came to light in 2017, when Uber was discovered to have been illegally using its 'greyball' software to help thwart government regulation. By geofencing government offices, credit card information associated with government officials, and social media, Uber tried to prevent its app from being used by government officials.

The fact that both these examples involve cars should give us pause. In the race to transform transportation by developing autonomous vehicles, electric cars and trucks, as well as new modes of transport, we can expect that many more transport companies will be tempted to use algorithms to act illegally. Trillions of dollars are at stake, so the potential rewards are immense. And we have very few safeguards in place to prevent it happening.

WHAT IS FAIR?

In handing over decisions to algorithms, we must be more explicit about what it means to be fair. Computers are perfectly literal when they interpret instructions – often frustratingly so. So if we are to instruct computers to act fairly, we must be very precise about what being fair actually is.

Let's go back to the COMPAS program – but to make the discussion less racially heated, let's ask what it means for a program like this to be fair to men and women. Justice should be blind, and any program like this should be blind to gender. But what does that actually mean?

There are several different types of fairness we could try to code into our programming. One simple measure of fairness is that the percentage of men predicted to reoffend should be the same as the percentage of women predicted to reoffend. But this is too crude. Women might commit less crime than men, which would lead to us locking up additional women or releasing dangerous men just to ensure the same percentage of men and women are on parole.

A better measure of fairness would be for the program's overall accuracy to be identical for men and for women. That is, the percentage of people incorrectly classified should be the same for both men and for women. Women would rightly be outraged if a greater percentage of women were misclassified, especially if more were misclassified as being likely to reoffend.

The problem with overall accuracy as a fairness measure is that correctly predicting those people who will reoffend may be more important than correctly predicting those people who will not reoffend. Releasing people who will reoffend may 'cost' more than not releasing people who won't. By lumping the two groups together, we suppose they are equally important. It also goes against Blackstone's ratio that governments and courts should err on the side of innocence. Sir William Blackstone, in his seminal seventeenth-century work, *Commentaries on the Laws of England*, proposed: 'It is better that ten guilty persons escape than that one innocent suffer.'

A third measure of fairness breaks apart these two groups. We might ask that the false positive and false negative rates for men are the same as those for women. The false negative rate is the fraction of people who reoffend who are predicted not to reoffend. And the false positive rate is the fraction of people who do not reoffend who are predicted to reoffend. Women would rightly be outraged if the false positive rate for women was higher than for men, and if, as a result, more women were being wrongly incarcerated. Again, false negatives may be more damaging to society than false positives. We may therefore wish to give greater weight to reducing the false negative rate.

A fourth measure of fairness cuts the prediction cake in the opposite direction. We might ask that the failure and success prediction error rates are the same for men and for women. The failure prediction error rate is the fraction of people predicted not to reoffend who actually do reoffend. The failure prediction error rate divides the number of people predicted not to reoffend who do by the number of people predicted not to reoffend. This compares to the false negative rate, which divides the number of people predicted not to reoffend who do by the total number of people who reoffend.

Similarly, the success prediction error rate is the fraction of people predicted to reoffend who don't. The success prediction error rate divides the number of people predicted to reoffend who don't by the number of people predicted to reoffend. This compares to the false positive rate, which divides the number of people predicted to reoffend who don't by the total number of people who don't reoffend. Women would again rightly be outraged if the success prediction error rate for women was higher than for men, and if, as a result, more women were being wrongly incarcerated. Again, the failure prediction error rate may be more important to society than the success prediction error rate, as releasing people into society who reoffend may be more 'costly' than keeping people in jail who won't reoffend. Those who are unfairly kept locked up might not agree, but we must somehow balance their freedom against the safety of the wider society. We may therefore want to treat the two error rates differently.

We could use other fairness measures, such as the ratio of false positives to false negatives, or the equal treatment of 'similar' individuals. But this is not important to our discussion. The take-home message is that *fairness can mean many different things*. There isn't one simple definition. Indeed, often there is an ongoing discussion within society about what sort of fairness should be sought in a particular context. And where there isn't such a discussion, there often should be. In handing over decisions about these matters to machines, we need to think carefully about what we want fairness to mean in the given setting.

TRANSPARENCY

There is also a vital need for transparency in machine decisions. We want machines not just to make fair decisions, but also to be transparent in making these decisions in order to build our confidence in their fairness. This is a major challenge for AI systems today. Popular approaches such as deep learning generate systems that cannot explain their decisions in any meaningful way. Decisions are often the product of being trained on more data than a human could look at in a lifetime.

Humans, of course, are also generally not very transparent. And we are notorious for 'inventing' explanations for our decisions after the event. But there is a fundamental difference. We can hold humans to account for their decisions. If my decision is especially poor and results in someone's death, I will face manslaughter charges. Machines cannot be held to account in a similar way. It is thus more important that machines be able to explain their decision-making.

Transparency will help to bring trust to systems. If a medical app recommends you need some dangerous chemotherapy, most of us would prefer a transparent system that can explain how it has decided that you have cancer, and why chemotherapy represents the best course of action. Transparency will also help correct systems when they make mistakes.

There are, of course, areas in which transparency might be a luxury. We might not insist that the control software to a nuclear power station explains why it is shutting down the reactor. We'll probably accept the inconvenience of losing power temporarily, if it means we can avoid the risk of a catastrophic meltdown.

WHOSE VALUES?

Once we start to program values such as fairness into our computer systems, we then face the challenge of deciding precisely *whose* values we should program. Of course, some will come from our legal system. For example, an autonomous car will need to follow whatever local driving laws are in place. In the United Kingdom, you can only overtake in the outside lane, and you must never turn when the traffic lights are red. In the United States, you can overtake in any lane, and you can sometimes turn when there are red lights.

Not all our values are given by precise laws, though. And even when they are, there are many laws that are meant to be broken. We are discovering, for example, that autonomous cars shouldn't always follow the road rules. A 2015 study from the University of Michigan's Transportation Research Institute found that self-driving vehicles have 9.1 crashes for every million miles they drive, compared with 4.1 crashes for cars driven by humans.[5] Although they were involved in more crashes, however, autonomous cars were rarely at fault. What may have indirectly caused many of these accidents is that they were following the law too precisely. Many of these accidents occurred when the autonomous car was rear-ended. If someone rear-ends you, they are almost always technically at fault. But braking hard to avoid going through a yellow light increases your risk of being rear-ended. Many human drivers commit minor transgressions of the law, such as continuing through a yellow light or exceeding the speed limit when overtaking. Some of these minor transgressions reduce the number of accidents. Autonomous cars will have to take account of, and perhaps even commit, the same sorts of behaviours themselves.

We will also need to program some values that may have little to do with actual laws. For example, the driving rules don't say much about the courtesies we show to other road users, or the driving customs we have developed. Does flashing your headlights mean the other driver should pull out of the intersection? Or that there's a danger ahead? Or that there's a problem with your car? Autonomous cars will need to understand and, when the situation demands it, perform such actions themselves. Sometimes these actions will involve difficult ethical choices.

TROLLEY PROBLEMS

Ethical dilemmas around autonomous cars have entered the public discourse in the form of 'trolley problems'. The classic trolley problem involves a runaway railway trolley. It requires you to make a difficult life-or-death choice. Here is the classic scenario.

There are five people tied to some railway track that the trolley is heading towards. You are standing between the people and the trolley, next to a lever. If you pull this lever, the trolley will switch to a siding. It sounds simple, except there is also a person tied to the railway track in the siding. You have two options: either you do nothing and the trolley kills the five people on the main track, or you pull the lever, diverting the trolley onto the siding, where it kills one person. What do you do?

There are many variants of the trolley problem involving men pushed into the path of the trolley, organs transplanted from one person to save multiple lives, and people locked up rather than killed. These variants expose ethical distinctions, such as that between action and inaction, between certain and expected outcomes, and between direct effects and possible side effects.[6] You can go online and solve such trolley problems yourself. The MIT Moral Machine lets you solve trolley problems.[7] It even lets you create your own ethical dilemmas for others to solve. The goal of the Moral Machine is to build a crowd-sourced picture of human opinion on how machines should make decisions when faced with moral dilemmas of this sort.

The Moral Machine is a neat example of the MIT Media Lab's skill at generating publicity. But it is very unclear whether, as some AI researchers have suggested, we should give machines such morals.[8] Even if the Moral Machine has collected the views of over a million would-be executioners, there are many reasons not to have machines replicate what these people have said. Answering questions on a website does not compare to gripping the steering wheel of a car and consciously running someone over. There will be people who deliberately answer perversely; I once went on the Moral Machine and tried out what happens when your decisions unnecessarily kill additional people. The Moral Machine doesn't collect demographic information, so there's no way to ensure that the sampled population is representative of a wider population. And even supposing it was representative, or could be made to be, do we really want machines to reflect some blurred average of society as a whole?

There are many arguments that by 2062 we should be holding machines to *higher* ethical standards than humans. Because we can. Because machines can be more precise than humans. Because machines can think more quickly than us. Because they don't have our failings.

We certainly don't want to bake into machines the very biases that we would like to remove from society. These are the very biases that the Moral Machine measures. And one final argument: we should hold machines to higher ethical standards than humans, because surely they can and should sacrifice themselves for us.

CORPORATE ETHICS

Corporations will likely be some of the actors most responsible for giving values to machines. This will prove challenging, as the evidence so far is that many corporations, especially technology companies, have lousy ethics. If we don't act to change this, this will be a major problem in 2062.

Many of these tech companies are based in California, once famed as a place to tune in and drop out of the capitalist rat-race. But most are funded by a lot of old-fashioned corporate and military money. Google used to have the motto 'Don't be evil'; it should have been a red flag that the temptation was there. It wasn't 'Make the world a better place' or 'Bring greater happiness to people'.[9]

Of course, these big technology companies have greatly enriched our lives. But we're starting to discover that there are some hidden costs to all those 'free' services. Indeed, we are starting to realise that their free products are not free at all. As they say, when the product costs nothing, often *you* are the product. These are companies with some of the largest profit margins on the planet. They are not giving their services away without getting a lot in return.

One of the more popular philosophers in Silicon Valley is Ayn Rand. Her dangerous blend of libertarian and capitalist ideas appears to have infected many in the technology sector. Disruption of any kind is seen as good. Government, on the whole, as bad. We can and must let the market decide. But the market is neither benevolent nor far-sighted. There are many areas in which it needs regulation to ensure that we all benefit, and that we achieve some common good.

I could offer many examples. It would be very easy, for example, to pick on a company like Uber. So let's find a different target. Let's consider Facebook, a technology company that is investing significantly in AI. In 2014 there was a storm of protest when it was revealed that Facebook was secretly manipulating whether people were happy or sad. Facebook ran an experiment suppressing positive or negative posts from 689,000 users' news feeds to see if they could make them happier or sadder. No ethics approval was sought from an independent ethics committee for the experiment, despite two researchers from Cornell University being involved in the study.

Now, if I want to run an experiment on members of the public, I have to seek approval from my university's ethical review board. I must get informed consent from the participants. I need to demonstrate that the risks are minor, and take steps to mitigate any potential harm. The Facebook study did none of this. Facebook assumed that users had given consent when they agreed to the terms and conditions upon joining. These terms and conditions are, of course, so general that no ethical review board would approve them. And neither before nor after the experiment did they say anything to the hapless subjects, as any ethical review board would require.

Perhaps this might be fine when you are running an A/B experiment to decide what shade of blue to use on a web page.[10]

But it is not acceptable when you are deliberately trying to make people sadder. And it's not acceptable, in my view, to allow a lower ethical standard for companies than for universities. Indeed, we should probably hold companies to higher standards than universities, as companies are primarily in pursuit of profit rather than of knowledge.[11]

Concern about other aspects of Facebook's behaviour is growing. As a second example, Facebook recently introduced Messenger Kids. This is an app designed for children aged six to twelve. The company's motive is clear: they need to find the next billion users. Catching children at a young age is the perfect way to do this.

But there is mounting evidence that social media can make people depressed, anxious and unhappy. Indeed, even Facebook has admitted that social media can be bad for people's mental health. So should Facebook be encouraging young people, at a very impressionable age, to use *more* social media?

In the United States, the *Children's Online Privacy Protection Act* (COPPA) was passed into law in 1998 to protect children under the age of thirteen. It has prevented social media companies from signing up children, as they would require parental consent to disclose any information about a child. Facebook argued that its new Messenger Kids app had been approved by an advisory committee of experts from the fields of child development, media and online safety. But *Wired* magazine later discovered that most of these experts had been funded by Facebook.

Should Facebook not be putting more effort, then, into *removing* those under the age of thirteen from its platform, rather than making it easier for them to come on board? Mark Zuckerberg has even vowed to fight to overthrow COPPA at some point.[12] In years to come, will we look back with nostalgia to those more innocent times, before we exposed our children to the roller-coaster of social media?

Facebook's mission statement is: 'Give people the power to build community and bring the world closer together.' In 2017 ProPublica discovered that the company's algorithms would sell adverts targeted at 'Jew hater' and other anti-Semitic groups. Facebook has sold job adverts that discriminate against older people, and has biased adverts for its own jobs in favour of young people. It's hard to see how such business activities build community and bring the world closer together.

ELIMINATING BIAS

It might sound desirable to eliminate bias, but it is not possible. If Amazon recommends you a book, match.com proposes a date, or monster.com suggests a new job you might like, it is bias that is preferencing one book, date or job over all the others. In fact, a large aspect of machine learning is concerned with deciding the most desirable type of bias to give a program. This bias, often called the inductive bias, is the set of assumptions used to predict outputs, given inputs not previously encountered.

Bias can even be desirable. We might want university admissions processes to be biased in favour of people from poor neighbourhoods. Or loan decisions to be biased towards those least likely to default. Or machine translating to be biased against the sexism in its language corpora. Or autonomous cars to be biased towards giving way to pedestrians and cyclists.

And tools do exist that can change the bias away from something unwanted and towards something more desirable. We can, for example, try to improve the accuracy of our algorithms. Perhaps we need to train on more data, or add additional features, or change the model to improve its accuracy. Another option is to blacklist certain answers. As we saw earlier, Google blacklisted 'gorilla' as an acceptable label for its Photos app. The problem with blacklists is that it is often hard to ensure completeness. Of course, you can flip the problem on its head and have a whitelist of acceptable answers. But then you might miss out on a lot of useful new answers.

Another way to deal with bias is to scrub features from the dataset which introduce some unwanted bias. If you don't want loan decisions to depend on race, then don't include race as an input. But simply eliminating race from the input isn't likely to be enough; as we have seen, there may be other features in the dataset, such as postcode, which correlate strongly with race. We can remove such correlated features, but removing too many features will likely impact on accuracy. We can also change the dataset itself. If the training set over-represents men, we might choose to increase the number of women in the dataset. Perhaps the dataset can be modified to have the same demographics as the wider population?

Finally, the last tool to deal with bias is awareness. There is no perfect way to detect and change biases in AI systems. But without an awareness that bias might be present, there is no possibility for change.

THE GOLDEN AGE OF PHILOSOPHY

When was the golden age of philosophy? Was it the time of Socrates, Aristotle and Plato, when many of the foundations of philosophy were laid? Or the time of Descartes, who is often dubbed the father of modern Western philosophy? Or perhaps it was during the time of Confucius and his disciples, many of whose ideas still influence us today? Do not do to others what you do not want done to yourself, for instance. I suspect, though, that the golden age of philosophy is just about to begin.

The next few decades could be a boom time for philosophy, as we make concrete many of the challenging ethical choices that trouble us. Given how literal computers are, we will have to be more precise than ever before about our values as we give AI systems the ability to make decisions that impact us. By 2062, every large company will need a CPO – a chief philosophical officer – who will help the company decide how its AI systems act. And the field of *computational ethics* will flourish, as we consider how to build systems which follow the agreed-upon values.

A friend asked me recently how to persuade their child not to study philosophy at university but something 'more practical'. My answer was to applaud their child's choice of subject. We desperately need more philosophers in business, government and everywhere else. Without them, it will be impossible to ensure that the AI systems of 2062 reflect human values. And to ensure ultimately that *Homo digitalis* is more ethical than *Homo sapiens*.

0007

THE END OF EQUALITY

E quality is one of the human values under threat due to technological change. Of course, equality won't actually end. Ever since society began, inequalities have existed. No society has ever been truly equal. People have always been born to greater wealth, and to better opportunities. But the brief period of decreasing inequality that followed the two world wars has ended, and inequality is on the rise once again. By 2062, we could see some very serious inequalities within our society. So perhaps the title of this chapter should be the somewhat less catchy 'The End of Decreasing Inequality'.

Economists such as Thomas Piketty have made a strong case that inequality increases in capitalist economies when the rate of return on capital exceeds the rate of economic growth. The owners of wealth, then, win out over those who own only their labour. Increasing inequality has been the case for much of our economic history. And inequality isn't restricted to the capitalist system. Communism hasn't performed any better in practice, favouring a privileged few while failing to lift those at the bottom.[1]

Other trends, such as globalisation and the never-ending global financial crisis, are likely contributers to this increase in inequality. Unfortunately, AI will increase inequality further, concentrating wealth and power in the hands of the technological elite – unless, that is, we take corrective action in the near future.

LIFE HAS NEVER BEEN BETTER

One hundred years ago, life expectancy in the United States, Australia and the United Kingdom was around fifty-five years. Today, it is over eighty. At one point my life expectancy as an adult male was increasing each year by an additional year. That was a trend I could live with.

Extreme poverty has fallen to under 10 per cent of the global population for the first time. Back in 1900, extreme poverty affected over 80 per cent of people on the planet. Education has been one of the major reasons for this change. Several hundred years ago, around 15 per cent of the population could read. Today 80 per cent of the world is literate. Even more promisingly, 90 per cent of the world's population under the age of twenty-five can read. This reduction in extreme poverty has had an immense impact. You're now more likely to die from obesity than from malnutrition.

Most of us don't feel it, but it is also the least violent time in history. The annual homicide rate in London has fallen from over fifty per 100,000 people in the fifteenth century to less than two per 100,000 today. And despite terrible genocides in Bosnia, Rwanda, Syria and elsewhere, the death rate from civil wars has fallen tenfold over the last fifty years.

But while life has been improving around the world for the very worst-off, the gap to those who were lucky enough to have won life's lottery is widening rapidly. The richest 500 people on the planet increased their wealth by over $1 trillion in 2017 alone. And the world's eight richest billionaires now control the same wealth between them as the poorest half of the globe's population. Life has never been better for most people – particularly the very rich.

THE WORST PLACE TO LIVE

The country where inequality is arguably most obvious is the United States. None of the thirty-five member nations of the Organisation for Economic Co-operation and Development is as unequal as the US, and none has experienced such a sharp rise in inequality. In the United States, the richest 1 per cent have seen their share of national income roughly double since 1980, from 11 per cent to around 20 per cent of the total.

To put this into perspective, the share of income in Denmark going to the top 1 per cent rose from 5 per cent to just 6 per cent during this period. In the Netherlands, there was essentially no increase from 6 per cent levels. I suspect it is no coincidence that Denmark and the Netherlands both often rank highly in studies of the best countries in which to live. There are some other nations which have seen significant increases in the income of the richest 1 per cent. Britain, for example, saw the share of incomes of the top 1 per cent rise from 6 per cent to 14 per cent, and Canada from 9 per cent to 14 per cent. But no other country has seen as large an increase as the United States. And none started from such an unequal base.

And it's not just the poor who are being left behind. People in the middle are not sharing in the increasing prosperity. According to the Economic Policy Institute, median hourly wages in the United States have barely changed for decades. In 2016 US dollars, median wages increased from $16.74 in 1973 to just $17.86 in 2016. With ever greater health costs and declining job security, many of those in the middle are justifiably feeling squeezed.

TRICKLE-DOWN ECONOMICS

An argument often made to encourage us to accept the fact that the rich are getting richer is that their wealth will 'trickle down' and improve the lives of everyone. There's also the argument that taxing the rich will stifle growth and innovation. There is little evidence to support either contention. Indeed, there is much that shows the opposite.

The International Monetary Fund's analysis suggests that increasing the income share of the poor and the middle classes increases growth, while increasing the share of the top 20 per cent actually decreases growth. When the rich get richer, the benefits do not trickle down to the poor. When the poor get richer, the rich do also.[2]

An interesting experiment in trickle-down economics took place in 2012. The Kansas governor, Sam Brownback, implemented a program of generous tax cuts for businesses and the wealthy, and less generous cuts for lower earners. Five years later, the state's economy was in a terrible state. Thousands of jobs were being lost annually. The state was slashing pension funds, and cutting money for universities, Medicaid and other services. In 2017 Kansas threw in the towel and reversed the tax cuts.

In the same period, California tried doing the opposite. In November 2012 the state's voters approved Proposition 30, which temporarily raised state income taxes for the wealthiest residents of California, and increased sales tax. The revenue was used to fund schools and pay down $27 billion in debt. California has since enjoyed some of the strongest economic growth of all US states. Of course, other factors – such as the large tech sector – have doubtless contributed to California's growth. But taxing the rich doesn't seem to have hurt.

LAST TIME WAS DIFFERENT

There was a period following the end of World War II when things were different. Inequality decreased and social mobility increased. The introduction of the welfare state, labour laws and unions, of universal education, as well as local changes such as the *Veterans Act* in the United States and the *National Health Service Act* in the United Kingdom, created the conditions for profound change, and what is now seen as a period of a rather unusual reduction in inequality.

These changes were driven by some large shocks to society: two world wars, the intervening Great Depression, and the looming threats of communism, the Cold War and the spectre of nuclear annihilation. Perhaps challenges such as the global financial crisis and global warming will provide the necessary shocks to reform society for the upcoming revolution brought about by AI?

I am not confident. Politicians have neither the bravery nor the vision to act boldly enough. And our political systems do not empower them to be brave and visionary. It will take much more than printing money to create the conditions necessary for a positive outcome. We need to consider radical changes to our welfare state, to our taxation system, to our education system, to our labour laws, and even to our political institutions. I am not confident that there is enough urgency in our discussions.

It is probably too late to prevent major climate change. We must now look to cope with its effects. Similarly, I fear we will not act quickly enough to prevent technological disruption from damaging society. In writing this book, one of my goals is to provide a wake-up call and urge more rapid change.

CORPORATE INEQUALITY

Wealth is not only concentrating in the hands of the rich. It is also concentrating in the bank balances of a few immensely powerful corporations. Again, if we do not act to prevent this, the outlook by 2062 will be bleak.

Digital markets are often natural monopolies. The winner takes it all. We only need and want one search engine, one messaging app, one social media service. And except in China, where competition was enforced, we do indeed have one dominant search engine, messaging app and social media service.

In the last quarter of 2007, the publicly listed companies with the largest market capitalisation were PetroChina, ExxonMobil, General Electric and China Mobile. Ten years later, the largest four companies were all technology companies: Apple, Alphabet (the parent company of Google), Microsoft and Amazon. Back in 2007 only Microsoft made the top ten.

Tech companies such as Google once argued that they had to remain competitive. A better start-up could come along at any time, and users would change their search engine in a heartbeat. But this is no longer the case. No other company has the data or the financial clout to compete with Google. A corporation like

Google can afford to pay billions of dollars to buy out any start-up that threatens its dominance. A few years back, Google was buying a company every week. And if the start-up refused to sell, Google would build a similar service and give it away for free, thus driving any competition out of business. David stands no chance against such Goliaths.

DEALING WITH GOLIATHS

Governments have often regulated to ensure competitive behaviour. While legislation to mandate fair prices can be traced as far back as the corn market in Roman times, the economies of scale brought about by the Industrial Revolution created a greater need for action. The first volley in this continuing war was the breaking up of Big Oil.

By 1900, Standard Oil controlled over 90 per cent of the refined oil in the United States. John D. Rockefeller was its founder, chairman and chief shareholder. He is widely considered to have been the richest person in modern history. In 1911, following a public outcry, the Supreme Court broke up Standard Oil into thirty-four smaller companies under the *Sherman Antitrust Act* of 1890.

Further volleys against Goliaths have followed. In 1911 the US Supreme Court took aim at Big Tobacco, breaking up the American Tobacco Company into four smaller firms. In 1982 the court took on Big Telecom, breaking up AT&T into seven regional

Bell operating companies, as well as the now much smaller parent company. Most recently, the Supreme Court has lined up Big Tech, going after Microsoft but with little success. Across the Atlantic, the European Commission has had more success dealing with anti-competitive behaviour in the technology sector. In 2017 the EU fined Google a record-breaking $2.7 billion for unfair competition.

In the United States, much of the focus of anti-competitive regulation has been on the prices paid by consumers. However, anti-competitive behaviour impacts more than just the immediate price. Markets often fail to price in externalities like the cost of pollution, especially in the short term. There's also a pressing need to regulate data monopolies. Unfortunately, even record-breaking fines do not seem to be having the desired impact on the behaviour of the Big Tech companies.

Other actions have also failed. In 2011 Google paid $700 million for ITA, a company that provides software for airline reservations. The Department of Justice approved the deal, provided that Google kept the software open to other businesses for at least five years. Google waited just two further years before announcing that it would close off access in 2018. Ted Benson, a former Google employee, wrote on Twitter: 'That's an entire ecosystem of airfare startups executed with the stroke of a pen.'

CORPORATE GREED

Technology companies often work in markets with amazing returns. Digital goods cost almost nothing to reproduce, and digital services can be scaled quickly and cheaply. Alphabet, for example, makes over 20 per cent net profit on its annual income of $110 billion. By comparison, Walmart makes less than 3 per cent net profit on its income of $485 billion.

Part of the wealth of these large technology corporations is gleaned from their unwillingness to pay taxes. A report published by the EU Commission in September 2017 found that a digital business in the EU with international operations typically pays an effective 10 per cent tax rate, compared with the 23 per cent rate paid by traditional companies. Many technology companies pay even less.

In 2016 Amazon paid just £15 million in tax on European revenues of £19.5 billion. That's not even 0.1 per cent of revenues. The revenues of Facebook UK in 2016 increased to £842 million from £210.8 million in the previous year, but somehow their taxes only increased from £4.2 million to £5.1 million. That's less than 1 per cent of revenues. Remarkably, the company's revenue increased fourfold but its tax rose by only a quarter.

Of course, it's not just technology companies that are paying little tax. Avoiding tax has become a game that many corporations play. For example, in its most recent Australian accounts, IKEA reported sales of A$1.16 billion. But after the accountants had worked their magic, IKEA is believed to have paid just A\$289,000 to the Australian Tax Office. One wonders why IKEA went to all the effort of selling over a billion dollars' worth of flat-pack furniture in Australia when it is clearly so unprofitable.

But it's true that technology companies are some of the most aggressive in avoiding tax. In Ireland, the European Commission found that Apple paid tax at a rate of just 0.005 per cent to the Irish tax authorities in 2014, far below the corporation tax rate of 12.5 per cent. The commission ruled that Apple should pay €13 billion in back taxes. As a result, we now have the bizarre situation where the Irish government is fighting the commission's ruling, trying *not* to receive billions of euros of taxes. The Irish government is playing a longer game, hoping Ireland can remain one of Europe's corporate tax havens.

The United Kingdom and Australia have both introduced special 'Google taxes' to try to force technology companies to pay a reasonable amount of tax. It only seems fair that these corporations should contribute something to the places where their revenues are generated. Indeed, if they had greater foresight, they would see that, ultimately, it is not in their own interest to drain the wealth of their customers.

The technology corporations don't need to generate such vast profits to continue to grow. Most pay no dividends, so have no need to be profitable enough to reward shareholders directly. Their profits are often used to buy back shares. This is a lazy option.

It says: 'We can do nothing useful with all this money.' And it has the effect of inflating the share price, which rewards those executives who hold share options. This needs regulating.

UBER'S DESTRUCTION

How did it all go so wrong? What became of the digital dream? Take taxis. A decade ago, in many places the market for taxis was not competitive. In a lot of cities you couldn't find a taxi on a rainy day. Taxi licences were often ridiculously expensive. Uber was supposed to fix this, but it ended up replacing one broken system with another.

There is so much to criticise about Uber. We have Uber drivers forced to live in their cars because they are paid so little. And Uber appears to have no qualms about breaking the law, or about spying on rival companies. Nor does it see a need to tell users that their data has been stolen. Putting aside all its bad behaviour, though, there is a much more fundamental problem with Uber: it is stealing most of the wealth out of the system.

The internet was supposed to reduce friction by letting us build digital markets that work more efficiently. Why is it so difficult to connect people who have cars sitting idle with those who need transportation so that *everyone* benefits? Is it fair that Uber takes so much of the value out of the system? Wouldn't it be better, for example, if we set up a cooperative in which the owners of the cars and their customers could share the generated value?

There are two reasons this hasn't happened. One is technological (and now fixable). The other is financial (and still waiting for a solution). The technological problem is that you don't want to get into a random person's car, or for a random person to get into your car. You therefore need a reputation system so that drivers and passengers can trust each other. Previously, a reputation system meant you needed to have a central authority that could maintain a record of drivers' and passengers' behaviours. And Uber has been that central authority. But this is no longer the case. With blockchain technology we could build a decentralised reputation system that cut out the need for a middleman like Uber.

This leaves the financial obstacle. Uber doesn't need to make money. It has raised and can continue to raise vast sums of money in the venture capital market. The ride-sharing market is therefore no longer a competitive one. It is not about which ride service is best. The ultimate winner is neither the consumer nor the taxi driver. The winner is simply the venture fund that has the deepest pockets. A cooperative can't compete against a business that doesn't need to make money. And certainly can't compete against a business that doesn't even need to break even, but will happily lose money. In 2016, Uber lost $2.8 billion on revenues of $6.5 billion. That's nearly a dollar out of every $2.32 coming in. Uber's backers are paying for around a third of every ride you take.

CORPORATE RESEARCH

You might be prepared to put up with naked capitalism, given all the benefits that corporations such as Google and Apple have brought to our lives. Think, for example, how many times a day you depend on Google, or on the iPhone in your pocket. But much of the technology improving our lives isn't the product of corporations. The internet was funded by the Defense Advanced Research Projects Agency (DARPA), a US government body. The World Wide Web was invented at the European Organisation for Nuclear Research (known as CERN), a physics lab funded by multiple governments. And much of the technology in the iPhone came out of government-funded research. Touchscreen displays, GPS, the internet and even the technology behind Siri were not paid for by the venture capitalists of Silicon Valley but by individuals' tax dollars.

Research requires a long view. It requires making many bets, many of which will not pay off. And it often contributes to the public good and not to a single company. Science is not something that is kept secret. As scientists, we publish in the open so that everyone can benefit. Of course, corporations contribute to the research ecosystem. And institutions such as the patent system help scientists publish and still receive the rewards their work deserves.

In recent years, big tech companies such as Microsoft, Google and Facebook have been strengthening their links to universities. Many of their senior staff are recognising that innovations often come from universities, not from corporate labs. They also recognise that almost all the researchers who staff the research and development labs of the tech companies come from universities.

It is true that corporations and not government funds have driven much of the recent boom in deep learning. But the foundations of this boom can be traced back to government funding. For many years, the Canadian Institute for Advanced Research funded Geoff Hinton at the University of Toronto and Yoshua Bengio at the University of Montreal. Hinton and Bengio were researching what was, at that time, the rather unfashionable topic of neural networks. The Canadians' far-sighted bet has paid off spectacularly, as Canada is now a hotbed for start-ups in deep learning.

THE MODERN CORPORATION

It is easy to forget that the modern corporation is a product of the last technological revolution, the Industrial Revolution. There are only a few companies in existence today, mostly banks and publishing houses, that go back over 300 years. Most corporations came into being much more recently. The average age of companies on the S&P 500 is just twenty years.

Ultimately, the modern corporation is a human-made institution, designed in part to permit society to profit from technological change. Limited liability lets the directors of corporations take risks without incurring personal risk. Equity and bond markets give corporations access to funds that allow them to invest in new technologies and markets. And the transferability of shares gives continuity to corporations so that they can grow over time.

Companies such as DuPont (founded in 1802), General Electric (1892), the Ford Motor Company (1903) and IBM (1911) are very clearly products of the Industrial Revolution. But a significant problem today is that although many corporations are greatly benefiting from recent advances in technology, much of the rest of society is not. Many tech companies are structured to give preferential treatment to their founders rather than to their shareholders. And even where founders are not privileged in this way, the structure of corporate governance lets CEOs act to maximise their own returns. These do not align directly with the returns due to shareholders, or more generally with the value returned to society.

To compound matters, some of these tech corporations have become as valuable and as powerful as small countries. Take Apple, which is currently worth around $850 billion and may soon become the world's first trillion-dollar company. Consider, for comparison, one of the wealthier but smaller countries in the world, Luxembourg. A rule of thumb in accountancy is that an asset is worth about ten times its annual income. The annual income of Luxembourg is its gross domestic product, which represents the total value of all the goods and services produced by the people of Luxembourg over the course of a year. This is about $60 billion. Based on this, you could say that Luxembourg is worth about $600 billion – or less than one Apple.

THE TWENTY-FIRST-CENTURY CORPORATION

Given that the modern corporation is a human invention, and in part a product of the Industrial Revolution, perhaps it is time to think about how we might reinvent the idea of the corporation to suit the coming revolution in work. In particular, how can we ensure that corporations in 2062 are better aligned to serve the public good?

There are several ingredients that might usefully go into the twenty-first-century corporation. The first is to reign in CEOs, and give better representation to workers and shareholders. Germany offers a good example of the benefits of giving workers a greater say. Companies in Germany with over 2000 employees are required to have a supervisory board, half of whom are workers at the company. This supervisory board sets executive wages, and hires and fires the CEO and other executive directors.

There is also a case for restricting the ratio of the pay of the CEO to that of the least well-paid workers within a company. In the United States, this ratio has increased roughly sixfold, on average, over the last three decades. Do CEOs work six times harder now? And while CEO pay has increased greatly in real terms, median wages have barely moved over the same time. We might also look to limit stock incentives offered to CEOs when corresponding incentives are not offered to other employees.

A second ingredient to help reform the modern corporation are incentives for mutual societies and cooperatives to grow. These might include: financial incentives such as lower tax rates; cheap government loans and favoured access to capital; business incentives such as a bias in government procurement in favour of such companies; and more relaxed liquidity requirements than for publicly listed companies (whose management might be tempted to be more risky, as they're gambling with other people's money).

A third ingredient are taxation reforms that compel corporations pay more tax in the places where they generate their wealth. This is ultimately in the long-term interest of everyone. Leaching wealth out of countries is not sustainable. Corporations benefit from having an orderly society in which to operate. Roads, hospitals, schools, transport and the like must all be paid for if these markets are to exist.

A fourth ingredient is the reform of employment law. With the growing 'gig economy', workers need to have greater rights, so that they can enjoy the protections that corporations have provided previously. Workers need to be able to be sick, to have babies, to look after elderly parents, and to retrain without falling below the breadline. Alongside this, unions need to reinvent themselves so they can help provide workers with greater rights.

A fifth ingredient is greater regulation of the data monopolies. Ultimately, this may mean that technology companies such as Alphabet and Facebook need to be broken up, as took place in the oil and telecommunications industries in times past. Before we get to this, less radical changes might also be considered. The big technology companies might simply be prohibited from buying new companies. And, as I discuss in the next chapter, we definitely need to think about new laws around data protection and data ownership.

FREE MONEY

Policy changes like these may be too small to ensure that all in society benefit from the AI Revolution. As with the invention of the modern welfare state at the dawn of the Industrial Revolution, we may need to consider more radical changes.

Universal basic income, a guaranteed and unconditional income for all citizens of a country, is one possibility. Interestingly, it attracts support from both sides of politics. Those on the Right see it as a way to reduce government bureaucracy, while for those on the Left it is a way to redistribute money to the poor. And it is favoured by many in Silicon Valley.

Giving everyone money unconditionally may seem radical, but in fact it is just an extension of what we already do. In many countries, you are educated at school for free. And in some countries you get free healthcare. Simply by being born in a country, you qualify for services worth thousands of dollars per year. Putting actual dollars in people's hands may seem a little more extreme, but we've been doing it implicitly for some time now.

The Swinging Sixties nearly brought a basic income to the United States. In 1967 Martin Luther King Jr wrote: 'I am now convinced that the simplest approach will prove to be the most effective – the solution to poverty is to abolish it directly by a now widely discussed measure: the guaranteed income.'[3] The next year, with young people around the world taking to the streets demanding a better future, 1200 economists wrote an open letter that was featured on the front page of the *New York Times* calling for a basic income for everyone. 'The country will not have met its responsibility until everyone in the nation is assured an income no less than the officially recognised definition of poverty,' they wrote. President Richard Nixon even tried to put this into practice. After some experiments with universal basic income in New Jersey, Pennsylvania, Iowa and North Carolina, Nixon put forward a bill in 1969 to end the ongoing War on Poverty. This would have guaranteed a family of four $1600 a year (equivalent to around $10,000 today). The bill was passed by Congress but was thrown out by the Senate. Nixon tried again the next year with the same result.

The looming threat of automation has now put the idea of a universal basic income back on the agenda. A number of experiments are underway in the Netherlands, Canada, Finland and elsewhere. They are designed to help answer questions about its feasibility. Will people still look for work? How will it impact on people's sense of worth? There are even fears that it could suppress wages, as employers might feel less need to pay a living wage.

One of the fundamental problems with all these pilot studies is their scale. None has been universal, or lasted for long enough to generalise the outcomes to a whole country and a whole generation of people. Nevertheless, the preliminary data from these (and earlier) trials has been positive. People don't seem to work less, health in these communities increases, and educational outcomes improve.

Major issues remain – perhaps the greatest of which is the cost of a universal basic income. In the United States, giving the 200 million adults of working age $18,000 per year each would cost $3.6 trillion. Funnily enough, this is the size of the annual US federal budget. But a universal basic income does not mean you can eliminate all other government spending. You still need to pay for roads, schools, hospitals and all the other public goods that people depend upon.

Less radical alternatives to a universal basic income have also been proposed. These include a higher minimum wage, stronger union and labour laws, the shift of taxes from labour to capital, and increased funding for job training and re-education. These alternatives have the advantage of requiring less radical change to society. But whether they will be enough, even if applied together, to cope with the changes on the horizon remains an open question.

GREEN SHOOTS

Technology companies are starting to wake up to their responsibilities. For example, Google announced in 2017 that it will invest $1 billion over the next five years in non-profit organisations that help people adjust to the changing nature of work. This is the largest philanthropic pledge to date from the company. However, supposing its profits continue to grow at present rates, this will cost Google less than 3 per cent of its profits over that five-year period. Paying corporation tax like other companies would return much more to the public.

As another example from 2017, Facebook announced that it will stop booking its European advertising revenues in Ireland, but start booking them in the actual countries in which they are earned. Critics have suggested that this move is unlikely to result in Facebook paying more tax. Nevertheless, it may signal the beginning of the end for aggressive tax avoidance by technology companies.

But perhaps the most promising green shoot comes not from a company but from a government. Over the last sixty years, governments in Costa Rica have focused not on growth but on providing universal access for its citizens to generous, high-quality social services, while at the same time protecting the environment. Abolishing the military and freeing up these resources for spending on hospital, schools and pensions has resulted in Costa Rica becoming a showcase for Latin America.

In 2016 Costa Rica spent 6.9 per cent of its budget on education, compared to a global average of 4.4 per cent. The money spent on healthcare has increased by around 50 per cent over the last twenty years, to 9 per cent of GDP. And over 70 per cent of this is government-funded. Costa Rica plans to become a carbon-neutral country by 2021. Over 98 per cent of its electricity is already generated from green sources. Its life expectancy of 79.6 years has exceeded that in the United States. Costa Rica has made itself a better place for its citizens by spending money on health, education and environment. Let's hope other countries are watching.

Tackling increasing inequality is not going to be easy. It will require boldness and vision. It will almost certainly require a greater redistribution of the profits that AI is bringing to the big technology companies.

At the World Economic Forum in 2018, the CEO of Google, Sundar Pichai, said that he was happy for Google to pay more tax, and called for the existing global taxation system to be reformed. That makes the future pretty obvious. By 2062, companies like Google should indeed be paying more tax, and this tax needs to be distributed globally.

0008

THE END OF PRIVACY

P rivacy is another human value under threat. Vint Cerf is Google's 'chief internet evangelist', and one of the architects of the internet. In 2013 he told the Federal Trade Commission that 'privacy may actually be an anomaly'. He justified this bold claim with the observation that '[p]rivacy is something which has emerged out of the urban boom coming from the industrial revolution'.

There's a certain truth to his claims. Back in the medieval age, life was a lot less private. Most of us couldn't afford to live in houses with separate living spaces and bedrooms. The Industrial Revolution lifted our standard of living and made some forms of privacy more possible. However, privacy is about more than having a room of one's own. It is also about having the privacy to discuss political change and to think dangerous thoughts. To vote anonymously. To practise the religion of our choosing. To live the lifestyle we wish. There are many other privacies that we have grown to expect.

By 2062, though, we will no longer be taking many of these privacies for granted. There is little that will escape the close scrutiny of a capable artificial intelligence. A vital question, then, is how we stop AI from compromising these privacies, much as George Orwell predicted in the canonical dystopian novel *Nineteen Eighty-Four*.

THE NEW OIL

Clive Humby, a British mathematician and the developer behind Tesco's groundbreaking Clubcard, is widely credited as the first person who compared data to oil.[1] Oil, of course, was the natural resource that drove much of the Industrial Revolution (pun intended). In 2006 Humby said: 'Data is the new oil. It's valuable, but if unrefined it cannot really be used. It has to be changed into gas, plastic, chemicals, etc to create a valuable entity that drives profitable activity; so must data be broken down, analysed for it to have value.'

In 2013 Abhishek Mehta, the CEO of Tresata, noted:

Just like oil was a natural resource powering the last industrial revolution, data is going to be the natural resource for this industrial revolution. Data is the core asset, and the core lubricant, for not just the entire economic models built around every single industry vertical but also the socio-economic models.

AI has been and will continue to be a major consumer of that data. Machine-learning methods such as deep learning currently require millions, if not billions, of training examples. If data is the new oil, machine learning is the refinery of those large datasets. By 2062, machine learning will undoubtedly be more like human learning and need fewer examples. Nevertheless, data will continue to be central to AI's success.

The analogy between data and oil should not be taken too literally, though, as there are some fundamental differences. Oil is a precious and limited resource. Data is neither precious nor scarce. Oil can only be used once. Data can be reused without limit. Unlike oil, data can often be used to generate more data. Piero Scaruffi, the author of *A History of Silicon Valley*, has written: 'The difference between oil and data is that the product of oil does not generate more oil (unfortunately), whereas the product of data (self-driving cars, drones, wearables, etc) will generate more data (where do you normally drive, how fast/well you drive, who is with you, etc).'[2]

But perhaps the biggest difference between oil and data is ownership. Countries quickly claimed ownership of the oil beneath our feet and under our seas. But much data today is privately owned. A few private data monopolies, notably Google and

Facebook, increasingly own most of our data. And while they are generating wealth from it, we — the producers of that data — are enjoying little of the value. In addition, all this data is putting our privacy under threat.

AI IS WATCHING YOU

In 2062 it will be a significant challenge to secure the privacy necessary to go about your private life. The *Economist* has estimated that Facebook alone has scanned, stored and can recognise 1.2 billion different faces. Think about that for a second. That's roughly one in six people on the planet. In a few decades, there will likely be a database somewhere aiming to contain every face.

Even our pets aren't safe: in October 2017 Google Photos started to recognise and label cats and dogs. And when Google sees your poodle, it will be primed to look for you nearby. So the next time you label a friend or a pet on social media, just remember that you are giving away not just the pet's identity but your friend's.

Silicon Valley may also have a good idea not just of who you are but also of how you will vote. Or of other intimate information, such as your sexuality. In 2017 a team from Stanford University demonstrated that they could predict how you vote simply using images from Google Street View.[3] Even a single Facebook like can provide enough information to predict voting behaviour.[4] Another team from Stanford University controversially claimed to have trained a machine-learning algorithm to tell apart the faces of homosexual and heterosexual people.[5]

There appear to be very few boundaries on the data that technology companies are willing to collect. Bruce Schneier, a privacy and security expert, observed that '[s]urveillance is the business model of the Internet'.[6] Al Gore put it even more succinctly when he called it the 'stalker economy'.[7] Why did Google think it should track your Android phone when you turned off your location and even removed your SIM card?[8] Why did Uber think it was okay to track your location five minutes after your ride was over?[9] Why did *Pokémon Go* think it should have access to your entire Google account on iOS, including your email and browsing history?

Of course, it's not just technology companies that are starting to invade people's privacy. States are also adopting new technologies to pry into our lives. The US state of Delaware, for instance, is putting 'smart' cameras into police cruisers to detect vehicles carrying fugitives, abducted children or missing seniors. Such uses might be unproblematic now, but what happens when a state starts using the same technology to track political activists or refugees? In China, police in Zhengzhou have started to test face-recognition glasses. These glasses can process 100,000 faces every second. You can't hide in a crowd of demonstrators when such technology is being used.

LINKED DATA

Even when a company has responsibly made the data they collect anonymous, they can fail. One of the problems is linking data from different sources. Individually, a dataset may give nothing private away. But when two or more data sets are combined, your privacy can be threatened. The Netflix challenge provides a good example.

In 2006 Netflix launched a $1 million competition to devise a better movie recommendation system. The company published 100,480,507 ratings that 480,189 users gave to 17,770 different movies. To protect users' privacy, Netflix carefully anonymised the data by removing personal details and replacing names with random numbers. But that didn't work. Researchers at the University of Texas at Austin were able to identify users in the Netflix dataset by matching the data against rankings and timestamps in the publicly available Internet Movie Database (IMDb). It turns out that, if you remove the most popular movies that we all like from the data, you can go a long way towards identifying someone from the combination of less popular movies that they like.

Netflix could have made the job of recognising users harder by removing a subset of the data, changing timestamps or introducing deliberate errors into the data. But even with partial data, data that has been perturbed or data with errors in it, it was still not too difficult to identify some of the users. It only took a small amount of non-anonymous data to strip the anonymity from the much larger but anonymous Netflix database.

Governments are well aware of the power of linking data. In 2015 the *Data Retention Act* came into force in Australia. This introduces a statutory obligation for telecommunications companies to retain particular types of metadata. For phone calls, this includes the number of the incoming caller, the location of the device and the unique identifier number assigned to the mobile phone. For emails, it includes the email address of the sender, and the size and date of the message.

On its own, there isn't too much you can do with such metadata, as it doesn't include the content of the call or of the email. But by linking it with other data, there is a lot that the authorities can work out – such as who you associate with and what you are doing.

OFFLINE PRIVACY

Even when we're offline, we are increasingly being tracked. One private company in the United States, Vigilant Solutions, has a database of over 2.2 billion photographs of numberplates and locations. Each month, it captures and permanently stores another 80 million or so records. Vigilant Solutions sells this data to thousands of law-enforcement agencies across the country that want to track people. It now has a contract with the Department of Homeland Security to provide real-time tracking of numberplates.

Not surprisingly, your shopping is also being closely tracked.

Google, for example, brings together marketing data from Ad-Words, Google Analytics and DoubleClick Search with location data from mobile phones to track when people visit a store. Each year, they track billions of visits to stores after users clicked on particular adverts. And Google has also started to connect store visits with purchasing data. Google's 'third-party partnerships' already capture approximately 70 per cent of all credit and debit card transactions in the United States. By 2062, we can expect companies like Google to be tracking all of our shopping, both online and offline. There will be a database recording every dollar you spend.

And once cities become 'smarter', collecting, analysing and acting on data about their inhabitants, we can expect offline tracking to be even more intrusive. There's really no way of opting out of such data collection. Everyone going about their business will be tracked. For example, in 2013 it was discovered that 'smart bins' in the City of London were tracking people's mobile phones.[10] Kaveh Memari, the CEO of the company making the smart bins, was very open about his firm's intentions: 'From our point of view, it's open to everybody, everyone can buy that data. London is the most heavily surveillanced city in the world … As long as we don't add a name and home address, it's legal.'[11]

His argument has a curious logic: because others are tracking people, we can too. Following a media outcry, the smart bins have been forced to stop tracking people's phones – for now. But by 2062, it won't just be bins tracking people. The whole city will be watching you.

BIG BROTHER @ HOME

Surveillance won't end when you get home. We are already seeing this with intelligent speakers such as Amazon's Alexa and Google Home. Although these only 'wake' when you speak to them, the reason they're able to do so is that they are *always* listening. And once they wake, they process your speech not on the device, but back in the cloud, on Google's and Amazon's servers. Google and Amazon only record a conversation once the device is woken. However, researchers have discovered how to hack them and record conversations at any time. This turns the speaker into a virtual wiretap. There's a reason people like Edward Snowden cover the camera on their laptop with tape, and put their phone in the fridge to block signals.

Police officials in Arkansas subpoenaed a customer's Alexa records in connection with a 2015 homicide at his home. Amazon refused to hand over the records, but before the issue could be tested in court, the customer's lawyer agreed to hand over the data. By 2062, we can expect all sorts of digital personal assistants to be testifying in legal cases.

It won't just be intelligent speakers that will invade the privacy of our homes. The next evolution of the internet is to the 'internet of things' in which we connect all the devices in our homes to the internet: our TVs, fridges, toasters, lights, even our plant pots. Most won't have a screen or a keyboard but will have voice interfaces. They will therefore have microphones permanently listening for commands. In Orwell's *Nineteen Eighty-Four* it was the government listening into our homes. In reality, the public is already paying private companies to put devices in our homes that can listen to our every conversation.

ANALOG PRIVACY

Some argue that the battle for our digital privacy is already lost. We have already irrevocably given up too much of our private information to Facebook, Google, Amazon and others. But we will shortly give up our analog privacy too. The problem is that we are connecting ourselves to smartwatches, fitness monitors and other devices that monitor our analog selves. We are revealing our geographical location, our heart rate, our blood pressure – and soon we'll add many other vital signs.

The benefits our obvious. The DeepHeart machine-learning app for the Apple Watch can detect atrial fibrillation, hypertension and sleep apnoea. It can even use your heartbeat to predict the onset of diabetes with a remarkable 85 per cent accuracy. This is all part of the promise that AI can make us healthier. But there are also risks. What if your health fund increases your premiums every week you skip the gym? Or if your employer fines you for working too slowly? Or if an advertiser shows you commercials that make your heart beat more rapidly?

With our digital selves, we can lie. We can pretend to be someone we are not. We can connect anonymously. But it is much harder to lie about your analog self. We have very little direct control over how fast our hearts beat or when our pupils dilate. Imagine what a political party could do if it had access to everyone's heartbeat? And we are giving this analog data away to private companies.

For example, when you sign up to use a FitBit device, FitBit collect lots of analog data about you on its servers: the number of steps you've taken today, the distance you've travelled, the calories you've burned, your current weight, heartbeat and location, as well as nearby WiFi access points, cell tower IDs, the computers you use and the webpages you visit. FitBit can tell a great deal about you from all this data.

As a second example, when you send your saliva off to Ancestry-DNA for genetic testing, you have to agree that you grant them 'a royalty-free, worldwide, sublicensable, transferable license to host, transfer, process, analyse, distribute, and communicate your Genetic Information for the purposes of providing you products and services, conducting Ancestry's research and product development, enhancing Ancestry's user experience, and making and offering personalised products and services'. And if AncestryDNA happens to use your DNA to develop a cure for a rare genetic disease that you possess, legally they can make you pay to use that cure. The AncestryDNA terms and conditions make it clear that 'you acquire no rights in any research or commercial products that may be developed by Ancestry using your Genetic Information'.

Actually, it used to be worse. Before a media outcry, Ancestry-DNA claimed a 'perpetual' royalty-free license. Once they had your data, there was no way for you to get it back. At least now you can ask them to delete your data and stop using it.

Unlike medical data collected by doctors and hospitals, analog data collected by FitBit or AncestryDNA is not protected by any patient/doctor or patient privacy legislation. A company such as FitBit or AncestryDNA can do pretty much what it likes with it. FitBit might work out who is having sex and try to sell them some viagra.[12] AncestryDNA might determine that you are at risk of Alzheimer's disease and sell your details to a local care home.

NON-HUMAN EYES

One of the arguments for allowing technologies like this to continue operating is that human eyes aren't looking over the data. Until 2017, Google's servers would read your incoming emails and use the information to offer personalised adverts. Of course, it wasn't a real person reading your emails, but an algorithm. Nevertheless, it can feel creepy. Google's executive chairman, Eric Schmidt, has said: 'Google policy is to get right up to the creepy line and not cross it.'[13] But the company's recent decision to stop reading emails suggests that it might have realised it had crossed that line.[14]

Previously, Google defended its actions in reading user's emails with this argument: 'Just as a sender of a letter to a business colleague cannot be surprised that the recipient's assistant opens the letter, people who use web-based email today cannot be surprised if their communications are processed by the recipient's ECS [electronic communications service] provider in the course of delivery.'[15] But the logic of Google's argument breaks down. You wouldn't expect a postal worker to read your letter as they deliver it. And you'd be a little disappointed if they read beyond the address on your postcard. So we should be surprised and disappointed that the *content* of our emails was being read while in the course of being delivered. As AI becomes better and better, we should be more and more concerned about its non-human eyes reading our correspondence.

THE GOOD APPLE

One company has tried to stand out from the rest in its respect for people's privacy. Apple's privacy statement makes this clear:

Apple products are designed to do amazing things. And designed to protect your privacy.

At Apple, we believe privacy is a fundamental human right.

And so much of your personal information – information you have a right to keep private – lives on your Apple devices.

Your heart rate after a run. Which news stories you read first. Where you bought your last coffee. What websites you visit. Who you call, email or message.

Every Apple product is designed from the ground up to protect that information. And to empower you to choose what you share and with whom.

We've proved time and again that great experiences don't have to come at the expense of your privacy and security. Instead, they can support them.

In support of such strong statements about privacy, Apple has resisted dozen of requests from the US government to help provide access to data on locked Apple devices. Even when one of these devices was owned by a terrorist. For this, I applaud them.

But when it comes to the choice between people's privacy and naked profits, Apple has acted less virtuously. In February 2018, to comply with new Chinese data laws, all of the data belonging to iCloud users on mainland China was moved to the servers of a company owned by the Chinese government. The terms and conditions of Apple's service were modified to give permission to this company to access the data.

This wasn't the first time that Apple bowed to Chinese pressure. In 2017 VPN software which allows users to access websites banned in China was removed from the country's App Store. It's clear that Apple will submit to pressure from the Chinese government in order to remain in this very valuable market. By comparison, Google has resisted many of China's attempts to censor their search results. As a result, Google has largely been kept out of the Chinese market. Unlike Apple, Google should be applauded for standing up to the Chinese and putting its principles before its profits.

SOCIAL CREDIT SCORING

Perhaps the most concerning premonition of our privacy in 2062 is the social credit scoring system being developed in China. By 2020, China plans to collect all information available online about companies and citizens in a single place, and then assign a score based on this that measures how 'trustworthy' they are. The goal is to 'provide the trustworthy with benefits and discipline the untrustworthy ... [so that] integrity becomes a widespread social value'.[16] Official documents about the scheme provide few concrete details, but have suggested that the 'untrustworthy' will be punished by restrictions on their employment, travel, housing and banking.

The pilot implementations now underway have done little to dispel concerns about the scheme. One of the most visible pilot projects is Sesame Credit, a credit-scoring scheme run by Alibaba. While Amazon has 310 million customer accounts, Alibaba is even larger, with nearly half a billion monthly users. It processes over 11 per cent of all retail sales in China. The details of how the Sesame Credit score is calculated are secret. But it takes into account five factors: purchases made using Alibaba's mobile and online payment platform Alipay, personal information, timely payments on bills, timely payment on credit cards, and your friends. Best not have untrustworthy friends!

Until now, the scheme has been more carrot than stick. For example, those with good scores can book hotel rooms and rent bicycles without a deposit. For a time, they could access the priority lane at Beijing Airport. And China's biggest matchmaking service promotes people with good credit scores. However, China has announced that, starting in May 2018, people with bad credit scores will be prevented from taking trains and planes. The potential for misuse of this system is immense, and China is of course not a country with a good human rights record.[17]

POST-SNOWDEN

China is not the only country to be worried about. In 2013 Edward Snowden revealed the existence of numerous global surveillance programs, run by the intelligence agencies of the United States, Australia, Canada, New Zealand and the United Kingdom. Emails, instant messages, and landline and cell phone conversations were all being tapped. The goals were unambiguous: 'Collect It All', 'Process It All' and 'Exploit It All'. And it wasn't just our enemies that were being targeted; law-abiding citizens of the countries doing the surveillance were also caught up in this immense dragnet. Not surprisingly, there was outrage. Such blanket surveillance likely violates the Fourth Amendment to the US Constitution, which prohibits unreasonable searches and seizures and requires any search warrant to be judicially sanctioned and supported by probable cause.

Nevertheless, I still cannot understand why so many people expressed surprise that their emails were being read. Email is the easiest form of communication to intercept. Email is already machine-readable. Unlike phone conversations, it doesn't need to be transcribed. Monitoring unencrypted emails is too easy and too tempting for states to resist.

Unfortunately, AI will only make it easier for states to surveil their citizens. Speech-recognition algorithms can simultaneously listen in to millions of phone calls. Computer vision algorithms can simultaneously watch millions of CCTV cameras. And algorithms that process natural language can read simultaneously millions of emails.

EUROPE'S LEAD

Europe offers some hope for privacy in 2062. In May 2018 the *General Data Protection Regulation* (GDPR) act came into force across Europe. The act's main goal is to give European citizens control of their personal data. It provides them with some basic rights over their data, such as a right to access it, and to erase it.

Perhaps the most relevant aspect of the discussion of privacy concerns the right to explanation. When an AI makes automated decisions, the act says that we have the right to 'meaningful information about the logic involved, as well as the significance and the envisaged consequences of such processing'. We have yet to see how the courts will interpret this. But it may ensure that European citizens get useful explanations of how an AI program comes to its decisions, as well as the ability to opt out of any such decision-making.

To gain consent to collect and use your data, the GDPR prohibits companies from using long, illegible terms and conditions that are full of 'legalese'. Consent must be clear and distinguishable from other matters, and provided in an intelligible and easily accessible form, using clear and plain language. It must also be as easy to withdraw consent as it is to give it.

The incentives to comply with the act are large. Organisations in breach of the GDPR can be fined up to 4 per cent of their annual global turnover, or €20 million (whichever is greater). We have yet to see the impact of these regulations, but they look like a good first step towards helping people preserve the privacy of their data.

DATA OWNERSHIP

The GDPR is only the beginning of the changes needed to preserve our privacy. How can it be that a company such as Facebook generates almost no content but owns it all? Wouldn't the world be a much fairer place if we owned our own data and got to say who could use it? And if this was a right, and not an 'opt out'?

At the Mobile World Congress in 2018, IBM Watson chief technology officer Rob High told a TechRepublic reporter: 'As with any new technology, it's really important that we be thinking now about how we do that ethically and responsibly. For us, that comes down to three basic principles. Trust, respect, and privacy ... Of course, privacy comes down to recognising that your data is our data.'[18]

You couldn't make this up! 'Your data is our data'? No, it's not. Your data is not IBM's data. Perhaps it was a slip of the tongue, but High's comments summed up the tech industry's sense of entitlement beautifully. It will likely need regulation, but by 2062, your data needs to be universally recognised as *your data*.

AI AS CURE

As is the case in many other areas, AI is not only part of the problem, but also a potentially significant part of any cure. There are a number of ways in which AI can help *preserve* privacy. One of the surest ways to keep hold of privacy is not to allow your data to leave your possession.

By 2062, we will have enough computing power on our devices that the computation can happen right there. Your smartphone will be smart enough to recognise your speech, understand your request and act upon it, without calling upon Google or any other service in the cloud. Your health monitor won't have to share your vital statistics with FitBit or anyone else. It will track your heartbeat and identify for itself when you need to see a doctor. By 2062, we will have AI privacy and security assistants sitting on all our devices. Their sole job will be to protect your privacy and defend your security. They will monitor all incoming and outgoing data, and intervene whenever your privacy or security is threatened.

Other technologies will also contribute to safeguarding our privacy. For example, quantum cryptography will be commonplace, offering even greater security to our data. And technologies such as differential privacy will be mature, letting us share data with others in society for the public good, but without giving up our own privacy. *Homo digitalis* could have far more privacy than *Homo sapiens*. Provided we have made the right choices, privacy will not be a historical anomaly. It will be a technologically given right.

THE END OF POLITICS

One area where privacy is needed most is in politics. We need private spaces in which we can explore alternatives to the current status quo. But even if we successfully use AI and other new technologies to keep hold of our privacy, politics will look very different in 2062. And depending on our choices, it may not be a 'better' different.

Over the last decade, we have seen a number of examples of how technology in general, and social media in particular, has started to change political debate. To begin with, it looked positive. The internet let us connect with other people in new ways, and gave a voice to many for the first time.

In 2011 we had a good preview of this positive potential, when an anonymous Facebook page titled 'We Are All Khaled Saeed' helped start the Egyptian revolution. Khaled Mohamed Saeed was a young Egyptian man killed in police custody in Alexandria in June 2010. The Facebook page about his violent death went viral and soon had over 100,000 followers. The page carried the first call for Egyptians to protest on 25 January, a national holiday recognising the Egyptian police. Tens of thousands of people took to the streets. After seventeen further days of demonstrations, with hundreds of thousands of protestors marching in Cairo and other Egyptian cities, vice-president Omar Suleiman announced that Hosni Mubarak would resign as president.

Other forms of social media also played a pivotal role in the uprising. One of the protestors, Fawaz Rashed, tweeted:

> We use Facebook to schedule the protests, Twitter to coordinate, and YouTube to tell the world. #egypt #jan25.

Many began to view social media as a powerful and positive force for political change. It wasn't only those in the centre of power who could speak out: anyone with an internet connection could now reach a large audience.

TECHNOLOGY AND POLITICS

Of course, new communication technologies have often been coopted for political ends. From the sixteenth century onwards, the printing press has been used to produce political pamphlets.

Thomas Paine's 1776 pamphlet *Common Sense* put forward arguments in favour of American independence, helping to unite the colony behind the idea of independence. It is widely considered to be the most important writing of the American Revolution.

More recently, radio brought politicians into people's living rooms. Winston Churchill wrote and delivered many memorable speeches during World War II that helped inspire the Allies' eventual victory. One of the most memorable was the speech he gave to the House of Commons on 4 June 1940, following the defeat at Dunkirk. Churchill's words gave courage to a nation that was expecting a Nazi invasion at any moment: 'we shall fight on the seas and oceans, we shall fight with growing confidence and growing strength in the air, we shall defend our island, whatever the cost may be ... we shall never surrender!'[1] Who cannot be stirred by Churchill's famous cadence?

And it's impossible to imagine politics today without television. The very first televised presidential debates, between Senator John F. Kennedy and Vice President Richard Nixon in 1960, sank Nixon's chances and helped catapult Kennedy into the presidency.

FAKE NEWS

It is not surprising that new communications technologies are having an impact on politics. And as many people are now getting much of their news from social media, one of the greatest concerns is fake news. After the election of Donald Trump in the United

States, Mark Zuckerberg, Facebook's founder and CEO, initially denied that fake news had played any role. 'Personally I think the idea that fake news on Facebook, which is a very small amount of the content, influenced the election in any way is a pretty crazy idea,' he said. 'Voters make decisions based on their lived experience.'[2]

Following mounting evidence to the contrary (and some renaming the site 'Fakebook'), Zuckerberg backpedalled in February 2017, publishing a 6000-word manifesto accepting that Facebook bore some responsibility. And one of the main solutions he proposed to deal with fake news was AI. Given the volume of posts, he argued, about the only hope for Facebook to filter content at a planet-wide scale is with intelligent algorithms.

Facebook's attempts so far to tackle fake news with human fact-checkers have had very limited impact. AI may help to detect fake news as Zuckerberg hopes – but it will likely also make the problem worse. Similar algorithms to those that detect fake news will be able to generate fake news. And as these algorithms that generate fake news get smarter, it will be harder and harder to tell real news apart from fake news. Truth will ultimately be the victim of this battle.

Facebook is not the only technology company that has been the subject of criticism. YouTube and Twitter have also been accused of distorting political debate. But Facebook was aware for many years of its power to change elections. This is especially worrying when its founder and CEO is being talked about as a future president of the United States.

FACEBOOK KNEW

In 2010 researchers from Facebook and the University of California at San Diego conducted an experiment on 61 million unwitting members of the American public during the US midterm elections. We know this because the researchers published the results two years later in the prestigious science journal *Nature*.[3] The goal of the experiment was ostensibly admirable: to increase voter participation.

The experiment was conducted on all people aged eighteen and over in the United States who used Facebook on 2 November 2010, the day of the elections. Users were divided into three randomly chosen groups. One was shown a message that 'Today Is Election Day'; others were shown the same message along with some thumbnails of their friends who had voted saying 'I voted'; and the third group was not shown anything. The researchers' results suggested that their interventions increased turnout by about 340,000 additional votes. This was around 0.5 per cent of the total number of votes cast. The Facebook experiment wasn't designed to change the outcome; it was simply designed to increase participation. In particular, there was no bias in the way users were encouraged to vote. Users for the three different groups were chosen entirely at random. What could be wrong with that?

Well, let's consider the Windsor-Orange 1 District for the Vermont House of Representatives. The 2010 election in this district was decided by a single vote. The outcome of the 2010 election in the Rutland 5-4 District for the Vermont House of Representatives was also decided by a single vote. Both elections were won by a female Democrat running against a male Republican candidate. In such close races, the Facebook experiment could have been critical.

Suppose for a moment that in 2010 Facebook had a younger and more female demographic in Vermont than the voting population of Vermont itself. This is not an unreasonable assumption: Facebook appeals most to adult women aged eighteen to twenty-nine. Now, suppose that younger women in Vermont were more likely to vote for a female Democratic candidate than for a male Republican. Again, this is not an unreasonable assumption. It follows, then, that increasing the voter participation of Facebook users in Vermont might easily have got one or two extra votes for the Democrats. As these elections were so tightly contested, this could definitely have changed the outcome, turning a probable Republican victory into the Democratic win that actually occurred.

It should not have surprised the researchers running the experiment that this could have happened. Thousands of different elections were held on 2 November 2010, some of which were surely closely contested. Indeed, Vermont was one of the more likely places to see a close result. The Vermont House of Representatives has relatively small electorates, making it more inclined to a narrow result. In 1977, 1986 and 2016 there were other districts for the Vermont House of Representatives that were also decided by a single vote.

Facebook ran further experiments to increase voter participation in the 2012 US elections. Less is known about these experiments, as they weren't written up in a scientific paper. Facebook claimed they selected voters at random and didn't focus on a particular group.[4] But, once again, Facebook is not a demographically balanced sample of the US electorate. Running an experiment on random Facebook users was again likely to have impacted the 2012 results.[5]

TARGETED CAMPAIGNS

Facebook's experiments to increase voter participation in the 2010 and 2012 elections were broad campaigns. They touched millions of voters chosen at random. More worrying, perhaps, is that social media can target small groups in a very focused way at very little cost. And it has been known for some time that Facebook can do this very well.

In March 2011 an online political campaign run by Chong & Koster, a digital ad agency, won an award for the Best Use of New Technology from the American Association of Political Consultants. The campaign ran for two months, starting in September 2010. It was limited to two of the most populated counties in Florida – Dade and Broward. These two counties had a combined population of 4.2 million people. The goal of this Facebook campaign was to reject a ballot proposition allowing larger classes in Florida's public schools. The campaign focused on groups that were most likely to be concerned about the proposition, such as parents and educators. A post-election poll showed there was a 19 per cent difference in the way people voted in areas where the Facebook ads ran versus areas where they did not. Those people in the areas exposed to the ads were 17 per cent more likely to vote against the proposition.

The campaign was remarkably cheap. The same amount of money would have paid for a postal campaign reaching less than 200,000 voters. For comparison, the digital ads on Facebook achieved 75 million impressions among people in key areas of Florida, with the average Facebook user in these areas seeing a targeted ad five times each day. Perhaps not surprisingly, the proposition was defeated. Facebook quickly learned about the digital ad agency's focused ability to manipulate votes. In August 2011, Facebook's official Government and Politics page discussed the campaign in glowing terms, concluding: 'Chong & Koster believes that the strategy of using Facebook as a market research tool and as a platform for ad saturation can be used to change public opinion in any political campaign. The agency has already applied the model for other campaigns.'[6] You can't be any clearer than this. Facebook can be used to change public opinion in *any* political campaign. These claims remain online on Facebook's Government and Politics page.

There are now companies making a profitable, if controversial, business out of influencing voters using highly targeted adverts, based on data extracted in dubious ways from social media and other sources. One such company that received much attention in early 2018 was Cambridge Analytica. Public concern about the company focused on how it acquired the personal information of US voters without their knowledge through Facebook surveys. The data was important, but in fact it was only part of the equation.

Rather than target audiences based on simple keywords, companies such as Cambridge Analytica have used sophisticated models of voters' personalities for their targeted political messages. Frighteningly, Cambridge Analytica claims:

> With up to 5,000 data points on over 230 million American voters, we build your custom target audience, then use this crucial information to engage, persuade, and motivate them to act ... with an unmatched understanding of your electorate, we will pinpoint the voters who will turn the tide in your favor, creatively engage with them, and drive them to the ballot box.[7]

If you do the maths, Cambridge Analytica has around a trillion data points on US voters. This wealth of information gave the company an unprecedented capability to pinpoint swing voters. Of course, all parties in a political campaign can use such technologies to try to swing the vote in their favour. But this comes at a real cost: a divided and polarised electorate.

Facebook's founder says he wants to bring the world together.[8] But selling political ads targeted at minority groups gives people the power to do the exact opposite: divide communities, pushing the world further apart.

Facebook has so far been a very active player in polarising our world. Therese Wong, a 'digital guru' for the Trump campaign, described in a 2017 BBC film how Facebook helped target voters.[9] She identified the desks in the San Antonio office of Cambridge Analytica where seconded Facebook employees sat helping Cambridge Analytica target swing voters. 'When you're pumping in millions and millions of dollars to these platforms, you're going to get white club treatment,' she told the BBC. 'Without Facebook, we wouldn't have won. I mean, Facebook really and truly put us over the edge.'

If we are not careful, politics in 2062 will be decided by such technologies. Big data mined from social media and elsewhere will be used by those with the smartest algorithms to gain power and influence. A figure as unlikely as Trump becoming US president or an outcome as divisive as Brexit may only be the start.

FAKE BOTS

It isn't only Facebook that is changing the nature of our political discourse. Other social media websites are also having a large influence. One that has been especially impactful is Twitter. Such is its power that there have even been calls to ban President Trump from the platform.[10] Actually, it's not humans but computers that have had some of the greatest effects on Twitter.

Donald Trump has around 48 million followers on Twitter. However, it is estimated that around 14 million of those are fake. The *New York Times* has similar numbers: of its 41 million followers, 11 million are estimated to be fake. Amusingly, Pope Francis does much worse than both Trump and the *New York Times*. Of the Pope's 17 millions followers, more than half – nearly 10 million – are fake. Appropriately enough, even worse is the President of the Russian Federation. Of Putin's nearly 2.5 million followers, around 60 per cent, or 1.5 million, are fake.[11]

One of the dangers of these 'fake bots' is that by 2062 it will be hard for humans to be heard above the sea of computer voices. Indeed, fake bots are already having an impact. In 2017 the US Federal Communications Commission (FCC) invited comments on the controversial issue of net neutrality. This is the idea that all data on the internet should be treated equally. You can't prioritise delivery of your emails over the upload of my YouTube video or the transmission of someone else's WhatsApp conversation. Of the 22 million comments received by the FCC on net neutrality, over 80 per cent came from bots.[12] People submitting comments were overwhelmingly in favour of net neutrality; perhaps unsurprisingly, the bots submitting comments were mostly against net neutrality.[13]

There is, however, one fake bot that I do applaud. A New Zealand cybersecurity firm, Netsafe, has set up a fake chatbot called Re:scam. Anytime you receive an email from a Nigerian scammer, you should forward it on to me@rescam.org. The chatbot then takes over replying to the scammer for you, doing its best to waste their time.

Computers pretending to be humans has a long history in AI. Indeed, Alan Turing's famous test of whether a computer could be said to think required it to emulate a human as proof. Every day we are asked to complete CAPTCHA tests to prove that we are indeed human.

But as AI becomes more capable, it is going to be harder and harder to tell computers and humans apart. In fact, we're already approaching that moment with Donald Trump. Bradley Hayes, a researcher at MIT's Computer Science and Artificial Intelligence Lab, used machine learning to build a twitter bot called @DeepDrumpf.[14] He trained it on transcripts of Trump's speeches. It now tweets much like the President himself:

20 Jan 2017
[We will be protected by God.] We don't win with healthcare. We can't afford it. It's very simple. Obamacare is a disaster. #inauguration

20 Jan 2017
Now, so there will be no misunderstanding, it's not my intention to do away with government. It is rather to make it generally terrible.

26 Sep 2016

Replying to @joss

[Lies], I mean are they prosecuted? Does anyone do anything?

It'll get me into the Oval Office. @joss @TheDemocrats

#debates #debatenight

FAKE POLITICIANS

Perhaps you weren't convinced by @DeepDrumpf? By 2062, however, you won't be able to tell the fake politicians from the real ones. You also won't be able to tell apart human politicians giving real speeches from those giving fake speeches. We already know that photographs can't be trusted. Software such as Photoshop can easily add people to or delete people from a photograph. Soon you won't be able to trust any audio or video recording either.

In 2016 Adobe previewed Voco, software for editing and generating audio. It has been called 'Photoshop-for-voice'. Beneath a person's speech, Vico shows a transcript that you can simply cut and paste. It couldn't be easier to change a politician's words. Other companies, such as CandyVoice and Lyrebird, are rushing to develop similar software tools.

Video will follow a similar path. Software already exists to past a new face onto a body in a video. Soon, you'll be able to drop a whole person into a scene. And it won't just be software that can manipulate existing video; we'll one day have software which can create completely artificial scenes that are indistinguishable from real video.

By 2062, you will no longer be able to believe anything you see or hear unless you're there in person. Unfortunately, unscrupulous politicians will take advantage of these new tools. They will simply deny the veracity of any genuine audio or video that surfaces and embarrasses them. Truth is set to be a very fungible concept.

THE FOURTH ESTATE

One of the most important duties of the press is to uncover truths. To expose corruption and lies. To keep politicians honest. By 2062, the media will be struggling to fulfil this fundamental and essential duty. The fight against fake news may well have been lost.

The internet has been a triple whammy to the practice of journalism. The first whammy was a loss of advertising income. Newspapers paid for journalism in part through the income generated by classified and display advertising. However, companies such as Google and Facebook have stolen much of that revenue. Similarly, radio and television have lost much of their advertising income to the web. In 2017 digital ad spending in the United States surpassed that spent on TV advertising for the first time.

The second whammy was a reduction in income from consumers of content. Newspapers have lost income as the public has begun to expect content to be delivered for free online. Many of us who used to buy a daily newspaper no longer do so. And while some news outlets such as the *New York Times* have replaced this income stream with digital subscriptions, many haven't.

In the United States, the weekday circulation of daily newspapers has nearly halved, from over 63 million in 1970 to under 35 million in 2016. Similar declines have been observed in other countries. In the United Kingdom, readership of the *Daily Mirror* has halved over the last decade, while newspapers such as the *Guardian* and the *Daily Telegraph* have seen their readerships fall by around 25 per cent. At the same time, television stations have lost a significant portion of their audience to online and streaming services. For instance, the viewing of broadcast TV in the United States among the lucrative 18- to 24-year-old age group has nearly halved over the last five years. The advertising dollars have followed these viewers away from television to digital services.

The third whammy has been a reduction in the number of journalists, as media companies cut costs to deal with their declining incomes. AI algorithms are increasingly being used to replace human journalists. And while these algorithms might do a good job of writing a short report, they are not able to produce long-form or investigative reporting.

There is some hope that part of this income will return. The internet giants are facing increasing calls to pay for their use of news content on their platforms. And bodies such as the European Union are considering how to make tech companies pay for the millions of news articles and links that appear on their websites.

These issues need to be resolved well before 2062 if we are to have a functioning fourth estate that keeps politicians in check.

PRESIDENT ZUCKERBERG

By 2062, leaders of technology companies will be important political figures. In 2017 Mark Zuckerberg announced that his new year challenge was to 'have visited and met people in every state in the US'. He then hired the chief strategist of Hillary Clinton's 2016 presidential campaign. He also had the certificate of incorporation for Facebook changed to permit him to hold public office. Not surprisingly, many commentators asked if we might one day see a President Zuckerberg.

Mark Zuckerberg was born in White Plains, New York, and so has every right, like any other natural-born US citizen, to run for president. Nevertheless, many have expressed concern about a person such as Zuckerberg seeking high public office. Unrestricted access to a platform like Facebook offers an immense advantage to a candidate in an election. Do we want to end up in a world where it is not the politicians with the best ideas who win, but those with the most data and the best algorithms? Most countries have limits on what can be given to and spent by candidates seeking office. Such rules prevent elections from being won simply by those with the most money. By 2062, we will need similar laws that limit the use of data and algorithms in elections.

We may also need laws that limit the influence of lobbying.

In recent years the technology companies have gone from having no presence in Washington to being some of the biggest lobbyists. According to federal records, in 2017 Google spent more on lobbying – $18 million – than any other company. Facebook was a little behind on $11.5 million, with Amazon on $12.8 million, Microsoft on $8.5 million, and Apple on $7 million. With the exception of Microsoft, each of these companies spent $2 or $3 million more on lobbying than they had in 2016.

POLITICAL CHOICES

The literary critic Roland Barthes observed that technologies are mythic. We tend to think of technology as if it's God-given, part of the natural order of the universe. We forget that it's the product of a specific political and historical context. Technology is not inevitable: it is what we choose it to be.

Take television. When the BBC was established, the British government decided that it would be a public good, funded by a tax and not paid for (and therefore driven) by commercial interests. This was a choice. I believe it was a good choice. We could also have decided seventy years ago that television was far too frivolous a medium for politics. Imagine how much better political debate would be now if it wasn't conducted via sound bites on TV? If politics was still conducted through serious articles in newspapers, and in public meetings?

By 2062, we might have decided that political adverts should be banned from social media. Or that political parties should only be allowed to broadcast their messages, and not to narrowcast them. Or that political bots should be banned from Twitter – or banned from the web completely. In a marvellous speech he gave in 1998, the humanist Neil Postman said:

> The best way to view technology is as a strange intruder, to remember that technology is not part of God's plan but a product of human creativity and hubris, and that its capacity for good or evil rests entirely on human awareness of what it does for us and to us.[15]

Postman was right. Technology is a strange intruder that we don't need to invite into all parts of our lives. We need to make some difficult choices about how AI is introduced into politics, so that, by 2062, it is improving, and not hurting, political debate. I have some hope that we will make the right choices, since we are already becoming aware of the great potential for its misuse.

0010

THE END OF THE WEST

A t the start of 2018, the four largest companies in the world by market capitalisation were all technology companies: Apple, Alphabet (the parent company of Google), Microsoft and Amazon. Software was well and truly starting to eat the world.[1] Google answers eight out of every nine search queries worldwide. This result would be even greater if it wasn't effectively locked out of China. The other three technology giants are dominant in their own spaces. Every month, one in four people on the planet uses Facebook. Microsoft provides the operating system used on more than 80 per cent of all laptops and desktops on the planet. And Amazon is responsible for nearly half of all e-commerce in the United States.

You might therefore guess that these four companies are set to dominate life in 2062, just as they dominate our online lives today. But, today's tech giants are starting to face some real competition. And it isn't coming from some amazing AI-powered start-ups. It's too easy for the four incumbents to buy out or stifle any young upstart. No, the competition comes from China. Technology companies such as Alibaba, Baidu and Tencent were born in the protected Chinese market, but are now innovating rapidly.

In 2017 the Alibaba Group announced plans to invest more than $5 billion in each of the next three years into research and development focused on AI, the Internet of Things and quantum computing. In 2018 Baidu filed an IPO for its Netflix-like service, which is expected to raise around $10 billion. Proceeds from the sale will be used to fund AI research and development. And in 2016 Tencent set up an AI Lab in Shenzhen with nearly 400 staff, part of the company's strategic focus on AI.

Even without such investment in AI, the Chinese tech giants are significant in size. Alibaba is the largest online retailer in China. It is currently worth over $500 billion. This compares to Amazon's market cap of around $750 billion. Alibaba, however, is growing faster than Amazon. Between 2012 and 2016, Amazon's sales doubled but Alibaba's more than tripled. We can therefore expect Alibaba to eclipse its US rival. As for Baidu, it is the largest search engine in China, and the fourth-most-visited website in the world. And Tencent owns the dominant social platform in China, WeChat. The company is valued at around $500 billion, just a fraction beneath the calculated worth of Facebook.

SPUTNIK MOMENTS

On 4 October 1957, the Soviet Union launched Sputnik, the first artificial satellite to go into low Earth orbit. It wasn't much to look at: a simple polished metal sphere around two feet in diameter. And it could do very little other than broadcast simple radio pulses from its four external radio antennas. But it woke the United States up to the threat of Russian technical prowess, and set off the race to the Moon.

In the race to build AI, DeepMind's two victories in the game of Go against expert human players look set to be 'Sputnik moments'. In this case, it wasn't the United States that awoke but the East. And it wasn't the race to the Moon that was kickstarted, but the race to build AI.

Shortly after South Korea's Lee Sedol was beaten by AlphaGo in March 2016, his nation's government created an ₩1 trillion ($863 million) fund for research into AI over the next five years. However, perhaps more significant was the awakening of the Chinese giant a year later. Following AlphaGo's victory against China's Ke Jie in 2017, the Chinese government announced an ambitious plan to lead the world in AI. The Chinese plan estimates that by 2030 AI will contribute ¥1 trillion ($150.8 billion) directly to industrial output, and ¥10 trillion ($1.5 trillion) indirectly via related industries.

AlphaGo's victories were sufficiently 'upsetting' that the Chinese authorities banned live streaming of the games. Go has a special importance in China, having been invented there over 2000 years ago. It is considered to be one of the four essential arts for aristocrats to master, along with *guqin* (a stringed instrument), *she* (calligraphy) and *hua* (Chinese painting). Not surprisingly, then, the fact that machines could beat the best humans at Go was a great shock.

CHINA'S PLAN

In July 2017, two months after Ke Jie's loss, the State Council of China issued the 'New Generation AI Development Plan'. The plan does little to hide the nation's ambition to use AI to gain economic and military dominance over the world. As President Xi Jinping reported to the 19th Party Congress in October 2017, China aims to become the 'science and technology superpower'. But the State Council's plan doesn't just seek economic and military dominance; it also describes an ambition to use AI to control China's own citizens. AI 'will significantly elevate the capability and level of social governance, playing an irreplaceable role in effectively maintaining social stability'.

Other parts of the plan are less troubling. Indeed, some aspects – such as its call for intelligent environmental protection and smart early-warning systems for public safety – are to be applauded. Similarly, it is pleasing to see plans to '[s]trengthen research on legal, ethical, and social issues related to AI, and establish laws, regulations and ethical frameworks to ensure the healthy development of AI'.

The State Council's initial goal is for China to be globally competitive in AI by 2020. As I will argue shortly, there are a number of metrics that suggest China will achieve this ahead of schedule. The plan also calls for China to make major breakthroughs in basic theories for AI by 2025, and to be leading the world in AI by 2030. I'm confident the Chinese will succeed in these ambitions. Even if they don't quite hit their targets, they surely will have by 2062. By then, China will likely have both the world's dominant economy and military.

For the last couple of decades, China's unusual mix of totalitarianism and strongly regulated capitalism has produced better growth than any Western economy. China's GDP doubled in the six years from 1998, tripled in the next six years, and nearly doubled again in the following six years. By comparison, the GDP of the United States grew by around one-third in each of these six-year periods. Over the eighteen years between 1998 and 2016, the GDP of the United States only doubled, while China's multiplied more than ten times.

China is, of course, a vast market. It has a population of nearly 1.4 billion people, more than quadruple that of the United States. This offers economies of scale beyond anything American and European companies can dream about. For instance, China is clearly the largest smartphone market in the world, with around 750 million units. This is roughly triple the number of the United States, and double that of Europe.

China is also adopting technology rapidly. In 2016 the volume of mobile payments in China more than doubled, reaching over $5 trillion. Electronic payments in China are predicted to grow ninefold, to $45 trillion, in the five years to 2021. Even today cash isn't accepted in some places in China. To put this into perspective, the United States saw just $112 billion of electronic payments in 2016. That's forty-five times smaller than China's.

China has other advantages in the race to build AI. For example, China has a more 'relaxed' attitude to privacy. The large tech companies and the Chinese state are able to share information more easily than in the West. As we've seen, China's social credit scoring system is a case in point. And while we should be worried about the impact of this for human rights, such data collection will only multiply China's advantage in the AI race.

SCIENTIFIC DOMINANCE

In 1999 the Chinese government began a program to massively expand university attendance. In that year alone, the number of students entering university grew by nearly half. For the next fifteen years, student numbers grew at a rapid rate, passing those of the United States in 2001; currently they are more than double the American numbers. By 2016, China was building the equivalent of nearly one university per week.

Many of these Chinese students study STEM subjects. The World Economic Forum reported that China had 4.7 million recent STEM graduates in 2016. This compares to just 568,000 in the United States. By 2030, China could have more than 40 per cent of all STEM graduates worldwide, compared with only 8 per cent in Europe and 4 per cent in the United States.

In addition to training more people in STEM, China has greatly increased its spending on scientific research. Over the past fifteen years, research funding in China increased more than six-fold in real terms, while funding in the United States and Europe grew by just 50 per cent. China now accounts for 20 per cent of total research and development expenditure worldwide. It is set to overtake the United States as the biggest spender in 2020.

More recently, both the Chinese government and Chinese businesses have started to make significant investments in AI research. Historically, China has not been a major force in this area. A decade ago there was little AI research taking place there. In 2013 I was on the governing board of the main inter-national AI conference when we decided to take it to China for the first time. Our goals were simple: to help kick-start Chinese AI research, and to tap into the immense potential China offers. We can already see that potential being realised. Just four years later, there were more papers submitted by Chinese researchers to the 2017 conference than by American and European scientists put together. In fact, Chinese researchers wrote over a third of all AI research papers worldwide.

Several other measures suggest that China has already caught up with the West, before its self-imposed deadline of 2020. CB Insights has reported that China had six times the number of patent publications using the keywords 'Deep Learning' than the United States, and five times more using the keywords 'Artificial Intelligence'.[2] It also reports that China's AI start-ups took 48 per cent of all dollars invested in AI start-ups globally in 2017, surpassing the United States for the first time.

AMERICA'S RESPONSE

The United States has dominated AI research from the early days of the field. Indeed, the term 'Artificial Intelligence' was coined in the United States for a summer workshop at Dartmouth College in 1956. It was there that many of the researchers who founded the field met for the first time and began tackling the challenge of building machines that think.

Not surprisingly, then, the United States has a plan to counter the threat of China winning the AI race.[3] In fact, the nation has a very credible plan that was made public in October 2016, nearly a year *before* the Chinese plan was revealed. And it's hard not to see many of the goals of the US plan reflected in the Chinese plan.

The US plan was prepared by the Office of Science & Technology Policy (OSTP), the department of the United States government that advises the president on the effects of science and technology on domestic and international affairs. The report followed a thorough consultation process of government, universities, industry and the public.

The US plan makes twenty-three recommendations. These range from opening up the government and its data for exploitation by AI, to prioritising long-term and basic AI research. There are also specific actions such as developing an automated air traffic management system that can accommodate both autonomous and piloted aircraft. The plan calls for transparency and fairness in the use of AI-based tools in both government and industry. Finally, it calls for the development of a single, government-wide policy, consistent with international humanitarian law, on autonomous and semi-autonomous weapons.

Unfortunately, the US plan's recommendations have been largely ignored. One month after the report was published, Donald Trump won the presidency. Staff numbers at the OSTP have now fallen by around two-thirds, and most of those who remain lack any science background. Unlike his predecessor, President Trump appears to have little interest in science and technology policy. The director of the OSTP has traditionally been the president's chief science adviser, but that position remains open. Indeed, there isn't even a nominee under consideration. Many other science and technology roles – including the United States Chief Technology Officer, and the director of DARPA – are also open. President Trump looks set to squander America's lead.

PLANS ELSEWHERE

Other countries have also responded to the Chinese AI plan. The United Kingdom is considered by many to be the birthplace of AI as a field of study. It was of course the British mathematician Alan Turing who wrote one of the very first scientific papers about building intelligent machines.[4] And the United Kingdom continues today to be a major player in AI research. Google's DeepMind was founded and continues to operate out of London, for instance.

In November 2017 Professor Dame Wendy Hall and Jérôme Pesenti published a review commissioned by the UK government's Business and Culture secretaries on how to grow AI in the nation. They made eighteen recommendations to improve the supply of data and skills, to maximise AI research and to support the uptake of AI. The UK government backed the report with a promise in April 2018 to invest $1.3 billion in AI research and development. With the challenges introduced by Brexit, I hope this will be enough for the United Kingdom to stay competitive.

India is set to have a larger population than China by 2022, so it's worth considering if it might pose a threat to China's growing economic dominance. At the start of 2018, India's finance minister announced in his budget speech that the government's premier policy think-tank would initiate a national AI program. The Indian government doubled the 2018–19 budget allocation to the Digital India program to ₹30.7 billion ($408 million) to support this initiative. While it's good to see India staying in the race, even close to half a billion dollars isn't going to be enough to win. In 2017 the Chinese city of Tianjin, which is only China's fourth-largest city by population, announced a $5 billion fund to support AI industry. Even if this is spent over a decade, a single city in China will be outspending the Indian government.

Several other countries have or are developing AI plans. Canada has committed a further $125 million to AI research. Even with plenty of local talent, this may not be enough to keep Canada in the race. France has an even more aggressive $1.85 billion plan. And the European Union is developing its own plan to keep Europe in the running. However, with Brexit approaching, Europe is set to lose its largest and most successful research community working in the field. This cannot help either Europe or the United Kingdom.

Finally, I come to Australia, which has yet to publish any AI plan. This is a great pity, as Australia has always had an academic community that has punched above its weight in AI research. Australia also has a very healthy start-up community, which is putting AI into practice in areas such as robotics, financial services, medicine and agriculture. I hope Australia's lack of an AI plan will be addressed in the near future.[5]

THE END OF NEOLIBERALISM

I have claimed that China looks set to win the AI race partly because the United States and other nations seem likely to lose. There will be a growing pushback against technology companies such as Google and Facebook in the next decade. This will hinder growth in the West and let China advance further in front.

Starting in the 1980s with Ronald Reagan in the United States and Margaret Thatcher in the United Kingdom, neoliberal ideas such as privatisation, austerity, deregulation, free trade and reductions in government spending have now been pre-eminent for several decades. But while these policies have produced economic growth for much of that time, there has been a cost: increasing economic insecurity and inequality.

Theresa May claimed in a speech to the Bank of England in September 2017 that '[a] free market economy, operating under the right rules and regulations, is the greatest agent of collective human progress ever created'. There is a very important condition to her claim: the market needs to be operating under the right rules and regulations. Without the right rules and regulations, monopolies will distort prices. Without the right rules and regulations, markets will not price in externalities, such as the true environmental cost. Without the right rules and regulations, markets can become overheated, resulting in price bubbles. And without the right rules and regulations, those with greater information will gain unfair advantages.

By limiting rules and regulations, neoliberalism exposes these fundamental problems within a market-based economy. And some of the most unregulated markets in operation today are those surrounding technology. It is therefore essential that we regulate these markets more forcefully. If the West is to keep up with China in the race to build AI, we need to embrace a kinder and more regulated form of capitalism.

0011

THE END

This book doesn't end quite yet. I didn't want to identify only the challenges facing us in 2062, challenges introduced in large part by machines that can think much better than us, challenges that *Homo digitalis* must solve. That would be far too pessimistic a way to end a story about what is likely one of our greatest creations.

However, we are approaching a critical juncture in human history. We face a bonfire of problems alongside the challenge of technological change – global climate change, the global financial crisis, the global refugee problem, to name just a few. Indeed, it sometimes seems that we only face *global* problems. And we have very few cards to play to deal with them. One of the few things we can do, if our grandchildren are to have better lives than us, is what our grandparents did many years ago. We need to embrace technological change. But we need to do carefully, so that it changes our lives for the better.

A mistake many people make is to think that the future is fixed, and that we'll simply have to adapt to it. That is not the case. The future is the product of the decisions we make today. We can therefore choose the future we want.

I don't pretend to know what the right choices are. It is not for me to say what the answers are; they are decisions that society as a whole needs to make. Nevertheless, I will try to identify some of the levers that we might choose to pull.

It may surprise you just how many levers I can identify. This is both good and bad. There's a lot we *can* do to ensure that the world of 2062 is better than the world of 2018. Equally, there's a lot we *must* do to ensure this. Above all, I am convinced that we cannot simply continue to let technology companies regulate themselves.

The tech companies have made some last-ditch efforts to try to head off the regulation of their sector; one is the Partnership on Artificial Intelligence, launched in September 2016.[1] However, there have been too many examples over the last few years in which technology companies have demonstrated that we cannot trust them to act in society's best interests.

It's not hard to see why we need greater regulation of the technology sector. The corporation is an old-fashioned institution that no longer aligns well with the public good. And technology companies, in particular, pose a challenge, given the disruptive effects that new technologies are having on our lives.

NEW LAWS

Data is one area in which regulation is needed. New laws are required to limit the collection and use of data, for instance. Europe has led the way with its *General Data Protection Regulation*. Similar legislation will be needed in other countries to protect their citizens' privacy. But it shouldn't end with better data-protection laws; we will need additional laws to control the capture and use of our data.

We might consider laws that fundamentally limit the ownership of data. Data about you should perhaps always be yours? We might decide that no one else but you should be allowed to own your heartbeat. Your DNA code, too, should be yours, and not something that a corporation can buy or sell. Most countries already have laws that prevent the sale of your physical parts – your organs and the like. We may need similar laws to prevent the sale of your digital self, especially without your permission or profit.

We might even consider legislating that data can only be owned by those who create it. With a platform like Facebook, this means users would own their posts, their friend lists, their messages and their events. Users would then be able to export their data to other social networks. In such a world, Facebook would need to keep its users happy or it would lose them.

Another law might be a statute of limitations on the use of data by any platform or company. Perhaps the limit should be ninety days? Maybe a year? But at some point, users must have the right to renegotiate the terms of how their data is used. And users should always have the right for their data to be forgotten.

In addition to laws concerning the capture and use of data, we might also choose to regulate the algorithms that act on this data. As we have seen, algorithms need not be fair or transparent. We might therefore have to insist that they are. And we might even need to prevent algorithms from being used at all in the making of certain decisions about people's lives and liberties.

To encourage innovation, platforms might also be required to open themselves up to competition. Some of the platforms have become too large to compete against. There must therefore be a healthy and competitive ecosystem *within* such platforms. Just as many states ensure that utility companies share the pipes and wires to our homes in order to create a (somewhat artificial) market for our business, we might have to legislate so that the digital platforms permit competition within their services.

Finally, we need laws that view platforms as being just like any other publishing format. Platforms must be liable for their content. This will force them to deal more actively with problematic issues that they have been avoiding, such as fake news or bots.

NEW CORPORATIONS

Another lever we could pull is to reform corporations. A fundamental challenge is that many new digital technologies are natural monopolies. And we don't have particularly good rules to deal with digital monopolies. Since the Reagan era, antitrust law in the United States has tolerated monopolies so long as they don't result in higher prices for consumers. Antitrust law has been and remains impotent to regulate companies which offer free services.

However, we now have a small number of technology companies dominating the digital space by offering free services. These companies dominate not just e-commerce, search and social media but also many other services, such as email, messaging, video and digital ads. They've even been allowed to increase their monopolies by buying rival and complementary companies. Google, for example, enlarged its monopoly into video by buying YouTube, while Facebook bought out Instagram and WhatsApp.

So where's the worry? How can a free service not be competitive, even if it is a monopoly? The problem is that these services hide the real cost to the consumer. When a service seems 'free', the actual cost is inevitably hidden. The impact of digital services on print journalism is a cost. Our addictive devices are a cost. Our loss of privacy has a cost. Thought bubbles have a cost. The stifling of technological change by the large tech companies buying out smaller and more agile competitors has a cost.

We might therefore need to break up the larger tech corporations to make the digital market competitive again. Well before 2062, for example, Alphabet will need to be broken into parts. Search. Email. Video. Mobile operating systems. No single company should be allowed to dominate all these spaces. Ironically, by setting up Alphabet, Google has made the job of breaking it into parts easier, undermining arguments that it needs to be kept together as one.

We might also need to prevent the tech giants from buying up or merging with their competitors. In 2012 Facebook bought Instagram for around $1 billion. And in 2014 it bought Whats-App, a competitor to its messaging service, for $19 billion. Well before 2062, deals like these should be prohibited. Instagram and WhatsApp were doing very well on their own before Facebook bought them. And it was probably Facebook, rather than the consumer, which benefited most from their sale.

The AI revolution might also require us to invent new types of corporation to ensure that we all share the benefits brought by technological change. Such corporations will align more closely with society's values. They will share more of their wealth with their employees and customers. And they will be able to take a long view, investing both in their employees and in the countries in which they operate.

Finally, we will need new taxes so that corporations pay their way in society. This may mean greater cooperation internationally to prevent corporations from simply playing one country off against another. It may also mean an increased use of taxes that are based on sales and turnover, as these are both harder to avoid and more direct in their return of wealth to the places it is generated.

NEW POLITICS

Political reform is a third lever we might pull in order to make the world of 2062 the one we want it to be. The Cambridge Analytica scandal of 2018 highlighted the corrosive effect big data is having on politics. To prevent political arguments being won by those with the best algorithms and the most data, we will need laws that limit the use of data to change people's political views.

Perhaps we should simply prevent the narrowcasting of political messages? If you have an attractive political idea, you can still broadcast it. But the micro-targeting of voters by machines should be outlawed. The use of computers as 'weapons of mass persuasion' should be banned. Social media companies, for example, might be prevented from selling advertisements based on any criteria except voting age and constituency. You won't be able to target unmarried millennial women or retired white men with divisive political messages. If Facebook wants to unite society, perhaps it should stop selling adverts in this way. And if it refuses to do so itself, we might have to legislate that it does.

We might even consider laws that prohibit completely the use of social media to win over voters. Imagine a world in which digital adverts were only allowed to be commercial, and not political?

A nice side effect of such a change would be that political parties would have to spend their money on traditional media, helping keep old fashioned journalism alive in our digital age.

We might also decide to ban bots from the internet entirely. It's hard to argue that bots make the internet a better place. And it would be easy to ban them. We would simply regulate that internet companies have to check the identity of any user, and fine them a percentage of their revenue when we discover bots stealing our attention. Human voices would take back control of the internet.

This still leaves the problem of fake content: fake news, fake video and fake audio. Technology will help in part. Technologies such as blockchain can help authenticate data, despite the decentralised nature of the internet. Education will also help. For example, Italy is now teaching children how to recognise fake news. Yet we may still need legislation. If platforms are forced to take responsibility for their content, then fake content will quickly be taken down.

NEW ECONOMICS

Economics is another important aspect of our lives that will have to change by 2062. Given the large impact that AI will have on work, there will be some radical new economies in play. As with the Industrial Revolution, it will be essential to protect workers if we are to ensure that 2062 is a better world for the many and not just for the few.

At a time when we need them most, unions in many countries appear impotent and behind the times. It's hard to imagine that the union movement will reinvent itself in time to deal with the AI revolution. If that is correct, then we'll have to look to other institutions to ensure that we all benefit from the coming technological changes.

We might, for example, legislate that companies have to retrain workers that are laid off before they can hire new staff. Such laws would be useful today. In early 2018, the Australian bank NAB announced it was laying off 6000 workers due to digitalisation, and hiring 2000 new staff with digital skills. Such callous, nakedly capitalist behaviour might be banned. NAB would instead have to reskill at least 2000 of the 6000 staff it planned to lay off, and find work for them – perhaps not even at NAB.

We might also require that companies regularly provide a minimum amount of education and reskilling for staff. To adapt an idea from Google, we might insist that 20 per cent of an employee's time is devoted to their personal development. This might sound idealistic – especially 20 per cent. But a company's greatest asset is often its people. How can investing in its own workforce not be a good long-term plan for any business?

Such ideas do little to protect those working in the 'gig economy'. We are already seeing abuses of these workers, and so we will surely need to introduce protections to prevent these from continuing. Both stick and carrot are possibilities. We might require that part-time employees get many of the same benefits as full-time employees, such as sick and parental leave. Equally, we might make it more attractive from a tax perspective for companies to employ people rather than subcontract their work.

We might also ensure that the balance of power is shifted in favour of those offering their labour. Abuses such as zero-hour contracts could be banned. And just as a company can choose which hours to offer, those being offered work must be able to decide which hours to accept, without fear of penalty. Governments will also need to step in and provide the security that companies once provided, so that even gig workers can have healthcare, be sick, take parental and carer leave, and retrain on the job.

Ultimately, these small levers may be inadequate to deal with the reduction in traditional work that occurs by 2062. We might therefore be living in economies where universal basic incomes have become commonplace. Less radically, we might be paying for much of the work done today that is largely unpaid, such as caring for the sick and the elderly, and raising children.

We might also be working a shorter week. With the robots doing much of the work, 2062 could be a time of leisure. We might be able to spend more of our time with our friends, families and communities. AI can give us this.

A NEW SOCIETY

By 2062 we might live in a much gentler society. If we value those who look after the young, the sick, the elderly and the disabled as much as – or perhaps even more than – those who are in traditional employment, ours will be a more caring society. Such caring jobs are not now, and perhaps never will be, jobs for robots. We must start valuing them more.

We might also see a flowering of creativity. As I suggested earlier, this could be the Second Renaissance. Even if robots can create arts or crafts, we will value more objects and experiences made by humans. And AI can provide the productivity gains that pay for more of us to be artists and artisans.

Supposing we have dealt with algorithmic bias, by 2062 we might also have a much fairer society. Machines will be making decisions without the historical and cultural biases that have distorted our past. Unlike humans, these machines might even be able to offer rational explanations for their decisions. We might have enacted regulations that require them to do so.

Society could also be more equal. When properly regulated, information technology in general, and AI in particular, can be a great leveller. Many more people will be lifted out of poverty. And many will be enjoying a more comfortable life. This, however, will require measures that ensure that all of us share in the benefits AI brings, and not just the owners of the technology.

Finally, society could be more peaceful. Supposing we have

limited the use of lethal autonomous weapons through legislation, AI could actually be saving and not taking lives: clearing minefields, helping provide humanitarian aid, reducing civilian casualties and protecting soldiers from harm.

If we make the right choices, AI promises to make life better – not just for the few but for the many. It can let us all live healthier, wealthier and perhaps even happier lives.

A BETTER FUTURE

In 2016 Barack Obama claimed that 'if you had to choose any time in the course of human history to be alive, you'd choose this one. Right here ... right now.'[2] I'll be honest: he actually said, 'Right here in America, right now.' But that was only because he doesn't live somewhere even better, like Australia.

There's a little rhetoric about Obama's claim. Around the world, life expectancy has increased greatly this century. However, more recently, life expectancy in the United States has begun to fall slightly, due to the opioid crisis. And while many people have been lifted out of poverty, inequality within many countries, especially in the United States, has been increasing. All in all, however, almost all of us are living much better lives now than our ancestors lived 100 years ago.

How did we get to be living such good lives? We did it by embracing science. You often hear it said that we live 'in exponential times'. Singularitarians would have you believe that exponential technologies will transform our world. And there's some truth to that. But perhaps the most important exponential changing our lives is one that is not mentioned often enough. This is the exponential advance of science itself. The bounty that this has given us is the reason that we live much better lives today than one hundred years ago.

To adapt the words of Sir Isaac Newton, science advances exponentially because scientists can stand on the shoulders of giants. We can exploit all the scientific knowledge that was discovered before us. And science advances exponentially fast, as more scientists are alive today than have ever lived in the past. Both are hallmarks of an exponential process.

However, it wasn't just science, and the technology it built, that changed our lives over the past century. We also made some significant changes to society to deal with the disruption that technological change brought to our lives. We introduced institutions such as unions, labour laws, universal education and the welfare state so that all of us shared in the prosperity brought by technological change. We should remember this as we enter another period of profound technological change.

Artificial intelligence will change our world dramatically. The world in 2062 will be very different from the one we live in today. We need, therefore, to think big about the changes we should make to society today if we are to ensure that the world of 2062 is the one we want.

Let's begin!

ACKNOWLEDGEMENTS

would like to thank my agent, Margaret Gee, and my publisher, Black Inc., who were instrumental in getting this book into your hands. Special thanks go to Chris Feik, my publisher; Dion Kagan and Julian Welch, my excellent and understanding editors; Kim Ferguson for a wonderful cover; Christina Taylor, Marian Blythe, Alison Alexanian and Wilson da Silva for generating some fantastic publicity; Nadia Laurinci and her team at Laurinci Speakers for managing all of my speaking engagements; and Sophy Williams for an amazing job on overseas rights.

There are many other people I'd like to thank.

My parents, who helped launch me on this path, dreaming about building artificial intelligence.

My many academic colleagues at UNSW Sydney, Data61 and elsewhere, for providing the intellectual environment and the support that allowed me to write this book, from the dean and my head of school to my many research collaborators and students.

And above all, I want to thank my family and friends, who give light to my every day, and who gave me the time to write a *second* book.

ENDNOTES

1. HOMO DIGITALIS

1   Contrary to popular belief, the Great Wall of China is not actually visible from space. But the pyramids of Giza can be seen from a low Earth orbit.

2   1 googol is 10^{100}, or 1 followed by 100 zeroes. The company Google was named after a misspelling of 'googol'.

3   In Australia, my last book had the title *It's Alive! Artificial Intelligence from the Logic Piano to Killer Robots*. But in the United Kingdom, in a suitably Brexit way, it had a different name: *Android Dreams: The Past, Present and Future of AI*. In the United States it was called *Machines That Think: The Future of Artificial Intelligence*.

4   Here are some fun facts about the year 2062. Elon Musk has predicted that we could have a city of a million people living on Mars by 2062. *The Jetsons*, the popular TV cartoon with robot maids and flying cars, was set 100 years in the future from its broadcast in 1962. For anyone who missed Halley's Comet in 1986, it should again be visible to the human eye in 2062. But not if the world has ended by then: in 1704 Isaac Newton predicted that the apocalypse would occur in 2060.

5   When I was a young boy dreaming about building machines that think, Arthur C. Clarke was one of my favourite science-fiction authors. Clarke once suggested that any sufficiently advanced technology is indistinguishable from magic.

6   We will talk about exponential changes shortly, but book production was one of the first exponential changes to have an impact on our society, one that has profoundly transformed that society.

7   Turing's universal machine is a more abstract and somewhat more mechanical device than the computers we have today. Nevertheless, it is no less powerful. It consists of a paper tape on which symbols are written, a head that can read this tape, write new symbols on the tape or move the tape left or right, and a box of electronics that performs various actions such as reading the tape, writing to the tape or moving the tape, depending on its internal state and the symbol most recently read. Turing first described such a machine in 1937. See Alan Turing, 'On Computable Numbers, with an Application to the *Entscheidungsproblem*', *Proceedings of the London Mathematical Society*, vol. 42, pp. 230–265.

8   Instructions for the Z80 and 6800 microprocessor are given as hexadecimal numbers, or base 16. Decimal numbers are base 10: once you go above 9, you go to 10, then 11, 12 and so on. In base 16, when you count above 9, you use A (=10), B (=11), C (=12), D (=13), E (=14), F (=15), and then 10 (=16), 11 (=17), 12 (=18) and so on. The 6800 microprocessor instruction DD is amusingly known by the mnemonic 'Halt and Catch Fire'. Before such microprocessors, computers were large and unreliable, and there was always a small chance that halting a computer would result in a fire.

9   Ironically, although computers are deterministic machines, computer science is one of the sciences in which experiments are least repeatable. Computers have become very complex, networked systems. As a result, it is often impossible to precisely recreate the conditions of a previous experiment.

10   The brain uses the most power of any of our organs. The heart, by comparison, uses less than 5 watts.

11   Yes, as I advised in my last book, you really can skip the endnotes completely!

12 Robert Gebelhoff, 'Q&A: Philosopher Nick Bostrom on
    Superintelligence, Human Enhancement and Existential Risk',
    The Washington Post, 5 November 2015.

2. THE END OF US

1 Garry Kasparov, 'The Day That I Sensed a New Kind of Intelligence',
   Time, 25 March 1996.

2 Elo ratings describe the relative skill levels of players in two-player
   games such as chess. The system is named after its creator, Arpad Elo,
   a Hungarian-born American physics professor. A player's Elo rating is
   updated whether a player wins or loses, and varies according to the Elo
   rating of their opponent. It is a little difficult to be completely confident
   about the Elo ratings of computer chess programs as they have typically
   played too few games under tournament conditions. Nevertheless, the
   gap between the best humans and best computer programs is now so
   large that there can be little hope left for humans.

3 On the first move in a game of Go, the white player can play any of 361
   positions (19 x 19); on the second, the black player can play any of the
   remaining 360 positions; on the third, the white player can play any of
   the remaining 359 positions; and so on.

4 All dollar amounts in this book, expect where specified otherwise,
   are in US currency.

5 In October 2017 DeepMind unveiled AlphaGo Zero. This improved
   upon the previous version of AlphaGo, as it was not given hand-trained
   features or shown expert human games. It was only given the rules of
   Go. It thus did not build on the thousands of years of human knowledge
   about Go, but learned everything for itself. After three days of playing
   itself, it was performing at a superhuman level. Like many of my AI
   colleagues, I was impressed. Computers could exceed thousands of years
   of human playing in just three days. I was even more impressed in
   December 2017, when the company unveiled Alpha Zero, an even more
   general version that could also learn to play chess and shogi (Japanese
   chess) at a superhuman level, from just the rules. However, it is not clear
   (and indeed it is unlikely, in my view) that these programs could learn

to play a very different type of game. Chess, Go and shogi are all two-player board games. Poker, for instance, introduces not only more players but also many new features, including uncertainty and human psychology. To win at poker, you have to deal with incomplete information about the cards, while in Go all information about the state of play is available to both players. In poker, you must also deal with an opponent's psychological tricks, such as bluffing. Neither the architecture of AlphaGo nor Alpha Zero is designed to deal with either of these features. To show domain independence, DeepMind would need to demonstrate that the same program could win at a wide range of different games, such as chess, poker and *StarCraft*. Even then, the Alpha Zero algorithm would still be limited to playing games.

6   AlphaGo was not the first artificial neural network that learned to play a game at human level. TD-Gammon was a computer backgammon program developed in 1992 at IBM's Thomas J. Watson Research Center. TD-Gammon played just slightly below the level of the top human backgammon players of the time. It explored strategies that humans had not pursued, and led to advances in our understanding of backgammon. Like AlphaGo Zero, it started from the rules of the game, and learned for itself how to play well.

7   The publicity that AlphaGo's victory gave Google in the valuable Chinese market likely paid for the millions of dollars that DeepMind spent developing AlphaGo. This may yet backfire on Google, though, as it appears to have motivated the Chinese to develop AI themselves. If one of the Chinese giants such as Baidu or Tencent wins the AI Race in front of Google, Larry Page and Sergey Brin may rue the day that they woke the Chinese giant.

8   In the aviation industry, a black box (which, incidentally, is never black – it's usually red or orange) records many internal statistics about the plane. In AI, a black box is a system where you only see the inputs and outputs. You have no insight into the internal states, and how it transforms those inputs into its outputs. The opposite of a black box is a glass box, which does offer a view into the internal workings.

9   The median prediction is the year by which 50 per cent of the surveyed group predicted computers would match humans. The mean (or average) prediction was an infinite amount of time in the future:

a small percentage both of the experts and of the non-experts predicted computers would never match humans.

10 There is, in fact, some evidence from IQ tests in the Danish and US militaries that average IQ scores may even have started to decline recently.

11 Moore's law is named after Gordon Moore, the co-founder of both Fairchild Semiconductor and Intel. In 1965 he described a doubling in the number of components on an integrated circuit every year. In 1975 he rounded this down to every two years. Moore's law has held for over fifty years. It is less well known that it has been officially dead for several years. Like every exponential trend in the real world, something has to run out. In this case, we are starting to run into quantum limits. The International Technology Roadmap for Semiconductors is the industry body that, as its name suggests, works out the roadmap to achieve Moore's law. In 2014 the ITRS declared that the industry's goals would no longer be a doubling every two years. And if it is no longer part of the plan of the major chip companies, then we can be sure it will not happen. No one will be spending the billions of dollars needed to build the next generation of chip fabrication plants necessary to shrink transistors further. Interestingly, Intel's goals now are to reduce power consumption so that we can have more computing power on our mobile devices.

12 See Martin Ford (2009) *The Lights in the Tunnel: Automation, Accelerating Technology and the Economy of the Future*, USA, Acculant Publishing.

13 See Jared Diamond (2005), *Collapse: How Societies Choose to Fail or Succeed*, New York, Viking Press.

14 Paul Allen, 'The Singularity Isn't Near', *MIT Technology Review*, 12 October 2011.

15 'The Cutting Edge: A Moore's Law for Razor Blades?' *The Economist*, 16 Mar 2006.

16 Jonathan Hall, 'Taking Another Look at the Labor Market for Uber's Driver-Partners', *Medium*, 22 Nov 2016.

17 H.G. Wells predicted the laser in *The War of the Worlds* (1897), and nuclear weapons in *The World Set Free* (1914).

18 The very respected Dutch computer scientist Edsger Dijkstra (1930–2002) famously once said that 'the question of whether

Machines Can Think ... is about as relevant as the question of whether Submarines Can Swim' (ACM South Central Regional Conference, November 1984, Austin, Texas).

19 See Stephen Omohundro (2008) 'The Basic AI Drives', in Pei Wang, Ben Goertzel & Stan Franklin (eds), *Artificial General Intelligence 2008: Proceedings of the First AGI Conference*, Frontiers in Artificial Intelligence and Applications 171, Amsterdam, IOS Press, pp. 483–492.

20 One of the least sophisticated methods of discounting the future is to consider a fixed time window. Rewards after this time window are simply ignored.

21 According to the historian Richard Rhodes, the idea for a nuclear chain reaction came to Leo Szilard as he crossed the street in Bloomsbury, London, the day after Rutherford had declared it would be impossible to extract energy from the atom: 'The stoplight changed to green. Szilard stepped off the curb. As he crossed the street time cracked open before him and he saw a way to the future, death into the world and all our woes, the shape of things to come' (see Richard Rhodes [1986] *The Making of the Atomic Bomb*, New York, Simon & Schuster). This nuclear chain reaction is one of the most dramatic examples of the power of exponential growth. One neutron splits an atom, releasing two neutrons. Those two neutrons split two new atoms to release four neutrons. Those four give eight, eight give sixteen, sixteen give thirty-two, and so on. Within ten steps we have released a thousand neutrons; twenty steps gives a million neutrons, thirty gives a billion, and forty gives a trillion. AI is now seeing the impact of similar exponential growth in computing power, in data, in the performance of algorithms and in funding flowing into the field. Like all exponentials, such growth won't continue forever, but while it does, the advances are impressive.

3. THE END OF CONSCIOUSNESS

1 David Chalmers (1995) 'Facing Up to the Problem of Consciousness', *Journal of Consciousness Studies*, vol. 2 no. 3, pp. 200–219.

2 David Chalmers (2010) 'The Singularity: A Philosophical Analysis', *Journal of Consciousness Studies*, vol. 17, no. 9–10, pp. 7–65.

3   On 9 October 1903, the *New York Times* published an editorial entitled
    'Flying Machines which Do Not Fly'. It rubbished the idea that humans
    would make flying machines anytime soon. 'The ridiculous fiasco which
    attended the attempt at aerial navigation in the Langley flying machines
    was not unexpected, except possibly by the distinguished Secretary of the
    Smithsonian Institution, who devised it, and his assistants ... It might
    be assumed that the flying machine which will really fly might be
    evolved by the combined and continuous efforts of mathematicians
    and mechanicians in from one to ten million years.' In reality, it didn't
    take a million years. Just sixty-nine days later, the Wright brothers
    demonstrated the sustained flight of a heavier-than-air aircraft over
    a windswept beach near Kitty Hawk, North Carolina. Mankind had
    found a very different way to fly than nature had.

4   For more discussion about possible quantum effects in the human brain,
    see Roger Penrose (1989) *The Emperor's New Mind: Concerning Computers,
    Minds, and the Laws of Physics*, New York, Oxford University Press.

5   CRISPR (pronounced "crisper") stands for Clustered Regularly
    Interspaced Short Palindromic Repeats. It is the basis for a powerful
    new technology to edit genes. *Science* named it as their breakthrough
    of the year in 2015. The Nobel Prize committee will surely be
    recognising its potential in the near future.

4. THE END OF WORK

1   Economists have been some of the loudest voices warning about
    the potential for technological unemployment. It is ironic, then, that
    the experts and non-experts in my survey most disagreed about the
    possibility of economists being automated in the next two decades.
    Four out of ten of the non-experts predicted that economists might
    be automated in the next two decades, while only one in eight of the
    experts made such a prediction.

2   See James Manyika, Michael Chui, Mehdi Miremadi, Jacques Bughim,
    Katy George, Paul Willmott & Martin Dewhurst (2017) *A Future
    that Works: Automation, Employment and Productivity*, McKinsey
    Global Institute.

3   This example was carefully chosen. The initial release of the HealthKit
    for Apple's iWatch in June 2014 did not track menstrual cycles.

4   In the United States, you have around a one in 114 lifetime chance
    of dying in a vehicle accident. To put this in perspective, you have a
    1 in 370 lifetime chance of being killed by a firearm, and a one in 9800
    lifetime chance of dying in an aircraft accident. You probably should
    be more worried about your car trips than your flights.

5. THE END OF WAR

1   Don't take my word for it that a fully autonomous drone is possible;
    the UK Ministry of Defence has also said it is possible today.

2   I will come back to the claims that autonomous weapons will be able
    to follow international humanitarian law, and will not commit atrocities.
    Contrary to the arguments of many of those in favour of autonomous
    weapons, I will argue that such claims are doubtful.

3   Weapons of mass destruction are often considered to be those capable of the
    indiscriminate killing of large numbers. Autonomous weapons need not be
    indiscriminate. Indeed, they could be the most discriminating weapons we
    ever make. However, the US Department of Defense defines weapons of
    mass destruction simply as 'capable of a high order of destruction or causing
    mass casualties'. It does not require such weapons to be indiscriminate.

4   To put this into perspective, image-recognition software today does
    a lot better than identifying a face correctly one out of ten times.
    Current accuracy is better than nineteen out of twenty times correct.

5   It is rather lost in the mists of history why the main AI conference is
    called the International *Joint* Conference on Artificial Intelligence. It is,
    however, the place to go to meet AI researchers from around the planet.

6   See Steven Pinker (2011) *The Better Angels of Our Nature*, New York,
    Viking Books.

7   Pope Francis is perhaps unaccustomed to coming third, but he was the
    second runner-up in the Arms Control Association's 2017 competition
    for Person of the Year. And I doubt he is used to being beaten by an
    obscure professor from Australia.

8   See Christof Heyns (2013) *Report of the Special Rapporteur on Extrajudicial, Summary or Arbitrary Executions*, United Nations Human Rights Council.

9   The 2017 United Nations Treaty on the Prohibition of Nuclear Weapons has been signed by fifty-eight nations, and ratified by seven of these. It will come into force when fifty states have ratified it. None of the nuclear weapons states or NATO members (excluding the Netherlands) has signed it, so we have yet to see its impact on nuclear disarmament.

6. THE END OF HUMAN VALUES

1   See Amit Datta, Michael Carl Tschantz & Anupam Datta (2015) 'Automated Experiments on Ad Privacy Settings: A Tale of Opacity, Choice, and Discrimination', *Proceedings on Privacy Enhancing Technologies*, vol. 1, pp. 92–112.

2   See Julia Angwin, Jeff Larson, Surya Mattu & Lauren Kirchner, 'Machine Bias', *ProPublica*, 23 May 2016.

3   Ian Tucker, '"A White Mask Worked Better": Why Algorithms Are Not Colour Blind', *The Observer*, 28 May 2017.

4   Dana Mattioli, 'On Orbitz, Mac Users Steered to Pricier Hotels', *The Wall Street Journal*, 23 August 2013.

5   With just eleven autonomous car crashes in the studied dataset, the margin of error on the accident rate is sufficiently large that autonomous cars could still be statistically safer than human-driven cars. However, you would hope to see a better average for autonomous cars as almost all the miles driven by the autonomous cars were in good weather. For details, see Brandon Schoettle & Michael Sivak (2015) *A Preliminary Analysis of Real-World Crashes Involving Self-Driving Vehicles*, The University of Michigan, Transportation Research Institute, Technical Report UMTRI-2015-34.

6   It is rarely observed that a modern form of the trolley problem was introduced over fifty years ago to discuss an ethical dilemma that still troubles many societies: the morality of abortion when a woman's life is at risk. See Philippa Foot (1978) *The Problem of Abortion and the Doctrine of the Double Effect in Virtues and Vices*, Oxford, Basil Blackwell (originally appeared in *The Oxford Review*, no. 5, 1967).

7   See moralmachine.mit.com.

8   'We submit that decision making can, in fact, be automated, even
    in the absence of such ground-truth principles, by aggregating people's
    opinions on ethical dilemmas.' See Ritesh Noothigattu, Neil Gaikwad,
    Edmund Awad, Sohad D'Souza, Iyad Rahwan, Pradeep Ravikumar
    & Ariel Procaccia (2018) 'A Voting-based System for Ethical Decision
    Making', *Proceedings of 32nd AAAI Conference on Artificial Intelligence.*

9   Following Google's 2015 restructure as the conglomerate Alphabet Inc.,
    the company motto changed from 'Don't be evil' to 'Do the right thing'.
    This suggests a more positive approach to corporate ethics. But I'm not
    aware of any journalist asking the obvious question: did Alphabet do
    the right thing and offer Spike Lee suitable compensation for its use
    of the phrase? His iconic 1989 movie *Do the Right Thing* is often
    listed among the greatest movies of all time. It is certainly on my list.
    Famously, Barack Obama and Michelle Robinson watched it on their
    first date.

10 A/B testing is a controlled statistical experiment where you compare
    two variants, A and B, to decide which is more effective. When she was
    head of product at Google, Marissa Mayer famously used A/B testing to
    trial forty different shades of blue to find the best colour for hyperlinks.

11 Given that universities are now more driven by profit than by the
    pursuit of knowledge, there's a rather ironic argument that, with regards
    to experimenting on the public, companies should indeed be treated
    like universities.

12 Michael Lev-Ram, 'Zuckerberg: Kids Under 13 Should Be Allowed
    on Facebook', *Fortune*, 20 May 2017.

7. THE END OF EQUALITY

1   Of course, there are other options apart from capitalism and
    communism. China's socialist market economy is an interesting case
    in point, which I'll discuss in more detail shortly. China has reduced
    poverty more than any other economy; however, inequality in China
    has also increased significantly.

2   See Era Dabla-Norris, Evridiki Tsounta, Kalpana Kochhar, Frantisek
Ricka & Nujin Suphaphiphat (2015), *Causes and Consequences of
Income Inequality: A Global Perspective*, technical report, International
Monetary Fund, June 2015, SDN/15/13.

3   See Martin Luther King Jr (1967) *Where Do We Go from Here:
Chaos or Community?* Boston, Beacon Press.

8. THE END OF PRIVACY

1   Address to ANA Senior Marketers' Summit 2006 at the Kellogg School
of Management, Northwestern University.

2   In *Humankind 2.0*, a book in progress; see scaruffi.com/singular/
bigdata.html.

3   See Timnit Gebru, Jonathan Krause, Yilun Wang, Duyun Chen,
Jia Deng, Erez Lieberman Aiden & Li Fei-Fei (2017) 'Using Deep
Learning and Google Street View to Estimate the Demographic
Makeup of Neighborhoods Across the United States', *Proceedings of
the National Academy of Sciences*, vol. 114, no. 50, pp. 13108–13113.

4   See Jakob Bæk Kristensen, Thomas Albrechtsen, Emil Dahl-Nielsen,
Michael Jensen, Magnus Skovrind & Tobias Bornakke (2017)
'Parsimonious Data: How a Single Facebook Like Predicts Voting
Behavior in Multiparty Systems', *PLoS One*, vol. 12, no. 9, e0184562.

5   See Yilun Wang & Michal Kosinski (2018) 'Deep Neural Networks
Are More Accurate than Humans at Detecting Sexual Orientation from
Facial Images', *Journal of Personality and Social Psychology*, vol. 114, no. 2,
pp. 246–257. There is much to criticise about this research. The study
looked at a very biased sample. It included only white people living in
the United States, between the ages of eighteen and forty. It considered
everyone to be either homosexual or heterosexual. The training and test
data used an equal number of homosexual and heterosexual images, while,
in reality, only around 7 per cent of this age group are homosexual. The
study claimed that the algorithm could distinguish between an image
of a homosexual or heterosexual man in 81 per cent of cases. However,
accuracy on a demographically balanced test set would be much worse.

And finally, what possible benefits could come from such a study? Developing software to recognise homosexuals carries immense risk. There are a dozen countries that have the death penalty for homosexuality. People dress and style themselves according to various cultural and sexual stereotypes. Doubtlessly, the machine-learning algorithm was picking up such clues. We don't need software to tell us this.

6   Bruce Schneier, '"Stalker economy" Here to Stay', *CNN.com*, 26 November 2013.

7   'Governments – that's one threat; businesses are also collecting more information than they should. We now have a stalker economy where businesses are finding out everything about you.' Al Gore, reported at the Southland Conference, 10 June 2014.

8   Shannon Liao, 'Google Admits It Tracked User Location Data Even When the Setting Was Turned Off', *The Verge*, 21 November 2017.

9   Amar Toor, 'Uber Will No Longer Track Your Location After Your Ride Is Over', *The Verge*, 29 August 2017.

10   Matt Warman, 'Bins that Track Mobiles Banned by City of London Corporation', *The Telegraph*, 12 August 2013.

11   Siraj Datoo, 'This Recycling Bin Is Following You', *Quartz*, 8 August 2013.

12   In 2011 the sexual activity of many of Fitbit users could be found in Google search results. However, this has now been restricted.

13   Eric Schmidt, Washington Ideas Forum, October 2010.

14   Google has stopped reading email in order to offer personalised adverts. However, it continues to read email for other purposes, such as adding calendar entries and suggesting automated replies.

15   Gregory S. McNeal, 'It's Not a Surprise that Gmail Users Have No Reasonable Expectation of Privacy', *Forbes*, 20 August 2013.

16   Stefan Brehm & Nicholas Loubere, 'China's Dystopian Social Credit System is a Harbinger of the Global Age of the Algorithm', *The Conversation*, 15 January 2018.

17 China lacked a credit rating system like that found in the United States, so it wasn't unreasonable for the Chinese government to want such a system to help tackle, for example, rampant corruption. But it has morphed into a far more troubling system.

18 Jason Hiner, 'IBM Watson CTO: The 3 Ethical Principles AI Needs to Embrace', *TechRepublic*, 2 March 2018.

9. THE END OF POLITICS

1 It is not widely realised that Winston Churchill's speech of 4 June 1940 was not recorded. Extracts were read by newsreader on that evening's BBC news broadcast. Churchill produced an audio recording in 1949, which many will have heard and likely supposed was from 1940.

2 Casey Newton, 'Zuckerberg: The Idea that Fake News on Facebook Influenced the Election Is "Crazy"', *The Verge*, 10 November 2016.

3 See Robert M. Bond, Christopher J. Fariss, Jason J. Jones, Adam D. I. Kramer, Cameron Marlow, Jaime E. Settle & James H. Fowler (2012) 'A 61-million-person Experiment in Social Influence and Political Mobilization', *Nature*, vol. 489, pp. 295–298.

4 'We've always implemented these tests [to increase vote participation] in a neutral manner. And we've been learning from our experience and are 100 percent committed to even greater transparency whenever we encourage civic participation in the future,' said Michael Buckley, Facebook's vice president for global business communications. Quoted in Micah L. Sifry, 'Facebook Wants You to Vote on Tuesday. Here's How It Messed With Your Feed in 2012', *Mother Jones*, 31 October 2014.

5 For the record, in the 2012 elections, the vote in District 27 for the New Mexico House of Representatives was a tie. After a recount, the Republican candidate was declared the winner by eight votes. It is quite plausible that Facebook's experiments in 2012 changed the outcome of some of the results, as they likely did in 2010.

6 See 'Case Study: Reaching Voters with Facebook Ads (Vote No on 8)', *Facebook*, facebook.com/notes/us-politics-on-facebook/case-study-reaching-voters-with-facebook-ads-vote-no-on-8/10150257619200882.

7   See Cambridge Analytica, 'About Us', ca-political.com/ca-advantage.

8   Mark Zuckerberg, 'Bringing the World Closer Together', Facebook post, 22 June 2017, facebook.com/notes/mark-zuckerberg/bringing-the-world-closer-together/10154944663901634.

9   See *Secrets of Silicon Valley*, Part 2: The Persuasion Machine, BBC Two, 13 August 2017.

10   In November 2017 Trump's Twitter account was briefly deactivated by a 'rogue' employee on his last day of work at the company. Some called for the employee to be nominated for the Nobel Peace Prize.

11   It's only fair that I report that, of my 1476 followers on Twitter (@TobyWalsh), forty-one are fake. I have absolutely no idea how forty-one bots got to follow me, and why they would bother.

12   Jane Wakefield, 'Net Neutrality Debate "Controlled by Bots"', *BBC News*, 4 October 2017.

13   In my view, about the only good argument against net neutrality is that the data generated by fake bots should be given less priority than that generated by humans!

14   The DeepDrumpf chatbot is named after a segment on the show *Last Week Tonight*, in which John Oliver encouraged people to rebrand Trump by his original family name of Drumpf.

15   'Five Things We Need to Know About Technological Changes' was an address given by Neil Postman to the New Tech '98 Conference in Denver, Colorado, on 27 March 1998.

10. THE END OF THE WEST

1   See Marc Andreessen, 'Why Software Is Eating the World', *The Wall Street Journal*, 20 August 2011. Andreessen is a co-founder of the venture capital firm Andreessen-Horowitz, which has invested in Facebook, Groupon, Skype and Twitter. Before becoming a venture capitalist, he was one of the founders of Netscape.

2   CB Insights, *Artificial Intelligence Trends to Watch in 2018*, 22 February 2018.

3 Preparing for the Future of Artificial Intelligence, National Science and Technology Council (NSTC), October 2016.

4 See Alan Turing (1950) 'Computing Machinery and Intelligence', *Mind*, vol. 59, no. 236, pp. 433–460.

5 I recently accepted a position to help the UAE government develop an AI plan. The reason I did was to cause embarrassment to the Australian government: not only does Australia not have a plan, but Australian researchers are even advising other countries on how to get ahead.

11. THE END

1 The 'Partnership on Artificial Intelligence to Benefit People and Society' is a technology industry consortium set up to establish best practices in AI as well as to educate the public about AI. It was founded by Amazon, Facebook, Google, DeepMind, Microsoft and IBM. A number of other companies, including Apple, joined shortly after.

2 Barack Obama, 'Now Is the Greatest Time to Be Alive', guest editorial, *Wired*, 10 December 2016.

BIBLIOGRAPHY

Robert M. Bond, Christopher J. Fariss, Jason J. Jones, Adam D.I. Kramer, Cameron Marlow, Jaime E. Settle & James H. Fowler (2012) 'A 61-million-person Experiment in Social Influence and Political Mobilization', *Nature*, vol. 489, pp. 295–298.

David Chalmers (1995) 'Facing Up to the Problem of Consciousness', *Journal of Consciousness Studies*, vol. 2, no. 3, pp. 200–219.

David Chalmers (2010) 'The Singularity: A Philosophical Analysis', *Journal of Consciousness Studies*, vol. 17, no. 9–10, pp. 7–65.

Era Dabla-Norris, Evridiki Tsounta, Kalpana Kochhar, Frantisek Ricka & Nujin Suphaphiphat (2015) *Causes and Consequences of Income Inequality: A Global Perspective*. Technical report, International Monetary Fund, June 2015.

Amit Datta, Michael Carl Tschantz & Anupam Datta (2015) 'Automated Experiments on Ad Privacy Settings: A Tale of Opacity, Choice, and Discrimination', *Proceedings on Privacy Enhancing Technologies*, vol. 1, pp. 92–112.

Jared Diamond (2005) *Collapse: How Societies Choose to Fail or Succeed*, New York, Viking Press.

Philippa Foot (1978) *The Problem of Abortion and the Doctrine of the Double Effect in Virtues and Vices*, Oxford, Basil Blackwell. (Originally appeared in the *Oxford Review*, no. 5, 1967.)

Martin Ford (2009) *The Lights in the Tunnel: Automation, Accelerating Technology and the Economy of the Future*, USA, Acculant Publishing.

Timnit Gebru, Jonathan Krause, Yilun Wang, Duyun Chen, Jia Deng, Erez Lieberman Aiden & Li Fei-Fei (2017) 'Using Deep Learning and Google Street View to Estimate the Demographic Makeup of Neighborhoods Across the United States', *Proceedings of the National Academy of Sciences*, vol. 114, no. 50, pp. 13108–13113.

Christof Henys (2013) *Report of the Special Rapporteur on Extrajudicial, Summary or Arbitrary Executions*, United Nations Human Rights Council.

Martin Luther King Jr (1967) *Where Do We Go from Here: Chaos or Community?* Boston, Beacon Press.

Jakob Bæk Kristensen, Thomas Albrechtsen, Emil Dahl-Nielsen, Michael Jensen, Magnus Skovrind, & Tobias Bornakke (2017) 'Parsimonious Data: How a Single Facebook Like Predicts Voting Behavior in Multiparty Systems', *PLoS One*, vol. 12, no. 9.

James Manyika, Michael Chui, Mehdi Miremadi, Jacques Bughim, Katy George, Paul Willmott & Martin Dewhurst (2017) *A Future that Works: Automation, Employment and Productivity*, McKinsey Global Institute.

Ritesh Noothigattu, Neil Gaikwad, Edmund Awad, Sohad D'Souza, Iyad Rahwan, Pradeep Ravikumar & Ariel Procaccia (2018) 'A Voting-Based System for Ethical Decision Making', *Proceedings of 32nd AAAI Conference on Artificial Intelligence*.

Stephen Omohundro (2008) 'The Basic AI Drives', in Pei Wang, Ben Goertzel & Stan Franklin (eds), *Artificial General Intelligence 2008: Proceedings of the First AGI Conference*, Frontiers in Artificial Intelligence and Applications 171, pp. 483–492, Amsterdam, IOS Press.

Roger Penrose (1989) *The Emperor's New Mind: Concerning Computers, Minds, and the Laws of Physics*, New York, Oxford University Press.

Steven Pinker (2011) *The Better Angels of Our Nature*, New York, Viking Books.

Richard Rhodes (1986) *The Making of the Atomic Bomb*, New York, Simon & Schuster.

Brandon Schoettle & Michael Sivak (2015) *A Preliminary Analysis of Real-World Crashes Involving Self-Driving Vehicles*, The University of Michigan, Transportation Research Institute, Technical Report.

Alan Turing (1937) 'On Computable Numbers, with an Application to the *Entscheidungsproblem*', *Proceedings of the London Mathematical Society*, vol. 42, pp. 230–265.

Alan Turing (1950) 'Computing Machinery and Intelligence', *Mind*, vol. 59, no. 236, pp. 433–460.

Yilun Wang & Michal Kosinski (2018) 'Deep Neural Networks Are More Accurate than Humans at Detecting Sexual Orientation from Facial Images', *Journal of Personality and Social Psychology*, vol. 114, no. 2, pp. 246–257.

INDEX

PRAISE FOR *IT'S ALIVE! ARTIFICIAL INTELLIGENCE FROM THE LOGIC PIANO TO KILLER ROBOTS*

'A whirlwind tour through the history and the future of AI – and why it matters to all of us. A must-read.'
—Sebastian Thrun, CEO of Udacity, Google Fellow and
Professor at Stanford University

'You've heard the hype, now read about the reality from one of the leading researchers in the field. In his elegant prose, Walsh describes the past, present, and future of AI – culminating in ten tantalising predictions.'
—Oren Etzioni, CEO of the Allen Institute for Artificial Intelligence

'Toby Walsh's story of how artificial intelligence evolved from the dreams of Alan Turing to a powerful technological force today is exciting, insightful and incisive. Will his predictions about how AI will change life as we know it in the coming decades prove equally dead-on? I, for one, would not bet against him!'
—Henry Kautz, past President of the Association for the Advancement of
Artificial Intelligence, Founding Director of the Institute for Data Science
and Professor at University of Rochester

'A comprehensive overview that avoids the hype and explains what AI can actually do, written by an expert practitioner of the field.'
—Peter Norvig, Director of Research at Google,
and co-author of *Artificial Intelligence: A Modern Approach*

'Toby Walsh is one of those rare individuals who combine a deep knowledge of AI technology, a serious interest in its economic and social implications, and a verve for lively and engaging writing. If you want real insights about the coming future of machines that think better and faster than humans in more and more domains, then you need to read this book.'
—Erik Brynjolfsson, professor at MIT and co-author of *The Second Machine Age*

'*It's Alive!* is stimulating, robust and, in its own way, reassuring.'
—Andrew Masterson, *Cosmos*

'Addresses a broad range of issues in clear and refreshingly non-technical language that is suitable for readers who are looking to explore the subject without being scared off by too much scientific jargon.'
—*Books+Publishing*

'When it comes to a discussion of where technology is heading, Walsh is worth listening to. He can also tell a good story. *It's Alive!* is an enjoyable read and fascinating stuff.'
—*In The Black*